PICTORIAL PROFILE

OF THE Holy Land

BY J. E. HOLLEY AND CAROLYN F. HOLLEY

FLEMING H. REVELL COMPANY

All of the pictures in this book are reproduced from the negatives in the Great Holy Land Library © by G. Eric Matson and are used by his permission.

INTRODUCTION

To READ ABOUT the Holy Land is good; to see it is better. In these pages, those of us never privileged to travel there personally may see it here as it has seldom been pictured before, and those fortunate enough to have known it at firsthand may have haunting memories stirred by this photographic record.

This book is, in the language of publishing, a "natural": it is the perfect combination of attractive subject and capable, reverent treatment. Dr. Holley, an author-illustrator, has wandered up and down the Holy Land for half a century, studying people and backgrounds and the lay and meaning of the land. He combines in this volume the artistry of a lens wizard with a scholar's love and understanding of his subject.

With the pictures are included a series of thumbnail maps and explanatory paragraphs and Scripture quotations, that all may be in proper place and perspective.

These pictures *live*: there is a vitality in them that gives the reader a sense of being there, on the spot. This is no photographer's holiday: it is the result of a lifetime dedicated to the task of making visible the footsteps of the Master in the homeland of three great faiths — the heartland of humanity.

It is, in every sense, a work of sacred art.

The Publishers

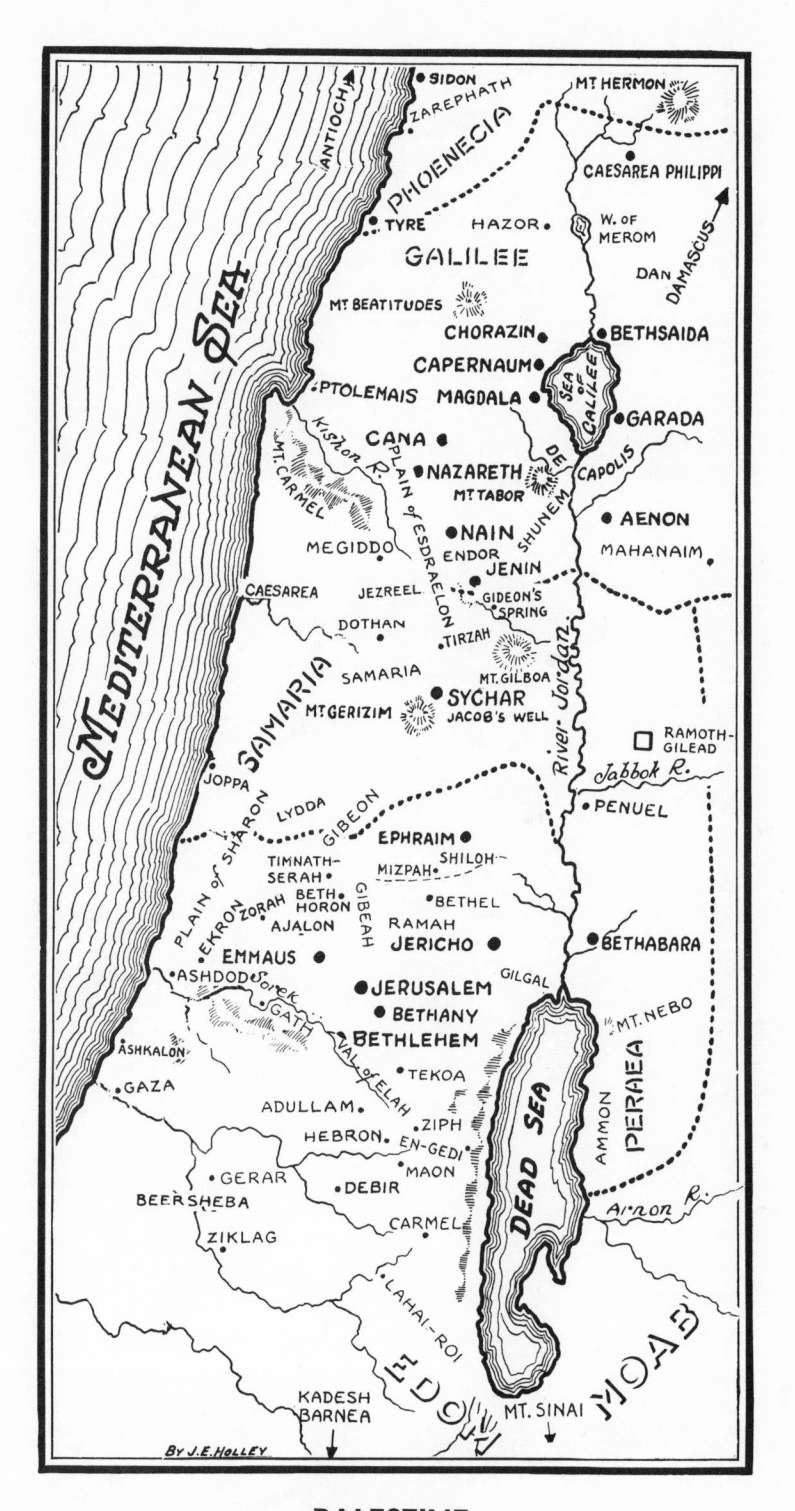

PALESTINE

APPROXIMATE SCALE

1— THE TRAVELER

The sages of old traveled at the rate of some two or three miles an hour, so it may have taken "The Wise Men from the East" many months to reach the "Babe of Bethlehem." But today, one may board a non-stop plane in the U. S. A. and land in the Holy City the same day. However, comparatively few have made the trip.

2— THE GLEANER

Among the thousands who have been asked: "Would you like to see the Holy Land?" few, if any, have said: "No." To tent with Abraham, stand on Pisgah with Moses, or accompany Jesus around the shores of Blue Galilee, in the courts of the majestic Temple, or dark Gethsemane, is sure to bring a thrill unlike any other one could imagine.

3— THE SHEPHERD

You may realize this ambition through the pages which follow, for they completely visualize this Sacred Land, all of it, and spread it out, section by section, place by place, before your very eyes. If you were to spend ten thousand dollars on a trip to the Holy Land, you would likely not see as much of it, nor from such vantage points.

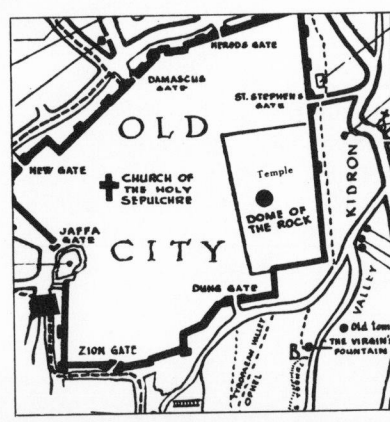

4— FIRST VIEW OF JERUSALEM

Now we begin our survey at Jerusalem, the Holy City, Zion, the place we have read about, and dreamed about so many times! So we will call this our "First View of Jerusalem." To the right is Zion with its "Church of the Virgin," "The Upper Room," and "Tomb of David." The road crosses the Valley of Hinnom, straight ahead, and leads past "The Citadel" to the "Joppa Gate." (Note black square on the chart.)

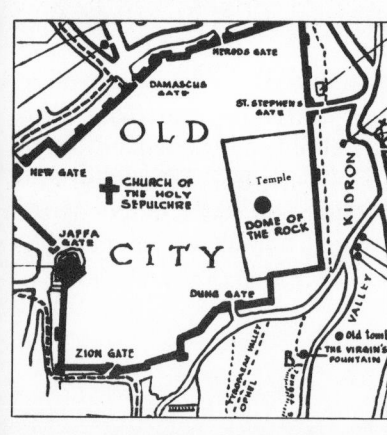

5— JOPPA GATE

This is the "Joppa Gate," main entrance to "David Street." Travelers from Egypt, Beersheba, or Joppa, enter the city through this Gate, and before the recent Jewish-Arab squabble, more people passed through it than all the others combined. Note the smaller door through the right side—this is called "The Needle's Eye," mentioned by Jesus. Matt. 19:24.

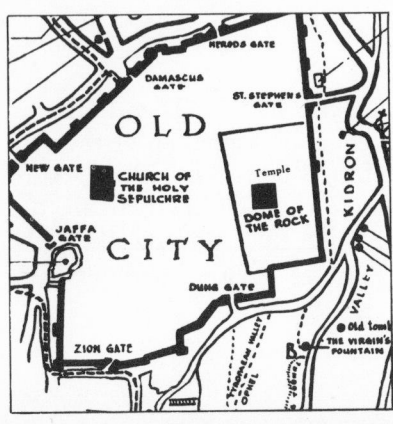

6— LOOKING ACROSS THE HOLY CITY

From the top of the west wall, we clearly see "The Church of the Holy Sepulchre." Beyond it is "The Mosque of Omar," on Moriah, where "The Temple" once stood, and looking down on it is "The Mount of Olives." In the valley between is "Gethsemane," where our Lord suffered and prayed. We will spend some time there when we get to it.

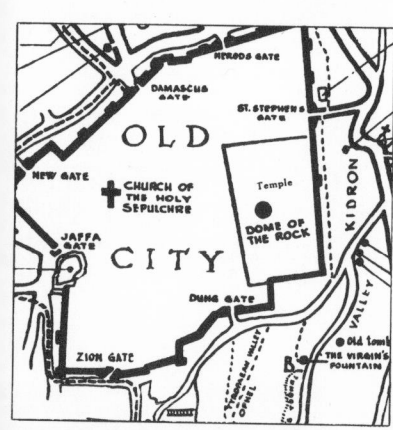

7— HOLY CITY FROM AIR

Now to complete the preliminaries to our study of the Holy City, let us take to the air and look down on it, so that we may understand it better when we get inside. Number 1 is Moriah (Temple site); 2, Holy Sepulchre; 3, Mt. Zion; 4, Gethsemane; 5, Joppa Gate and David's Tower; 6, Siloam Village and Hill of Evil Counsel; the dark streaks marked 7, Gorge of Hinnom (left), and 8, (right) is the Kedron Valley.

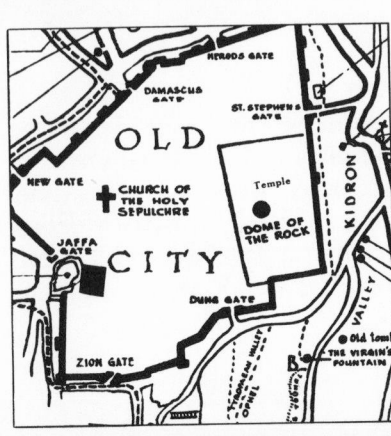

8— DAVID'S TOWER

Here we begin a trip around the city—outside. Immediately adjacent to the "Joppa Gate" (inside) is "David's Tower," which may have been constructed by Hiram of Tyre, David's personal friend. It was no doubt occupied first by David himself; but in Jesus' day it was probably used to lodge Potentates who were visiting Jerusalem on official business.

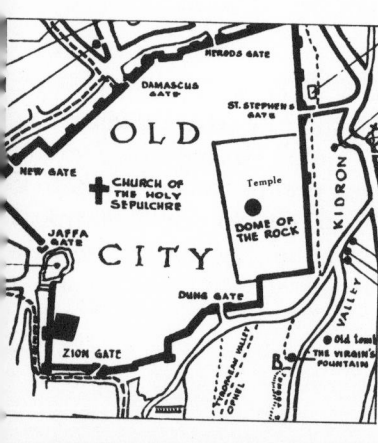

9— THE CITADEL

As a kind of extension to the Tower is "The Citadel," (outside) built to protect the city, but a single piece of modern artillery would make a shambles of it in one second. A bit later we will begin our trip to Bethlehem by this very road. Over the bank, at our feet, behind us, is "The Pool of Gehon," which, for years, was used as a market-place.

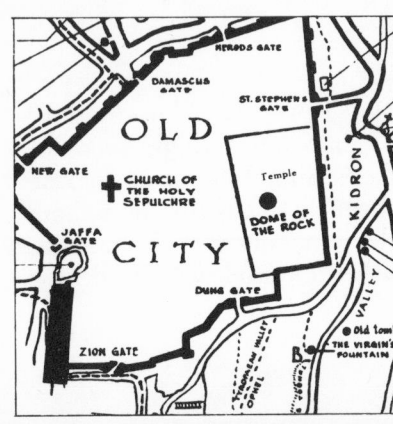

10— ZION FROM GEHON

And here is the empty Pool and the Market Place. At the top, left, is "The Citadel," and at the top of the ridge, the walls of Zion. The road leads on to the right (south), and then on around the Gorge of Hinnom. In fact, this is the head of "The Hinnom Valley" and in the next picture we will see how it connects with it.

11— HINNOM LOOKING EAST

And here it is, a kind of evil place, called "Gehenna, or
Hell." The distant hill is "Evil Counsel," where Solomon
housed his thousand wives. The god, Moloch, was located
in the valley, and mothers sacrificed their living infants
to him. (I Kings 10:7.) Judas contracted to betray the
Master in this gorge, and later hung himself from the cliffs.

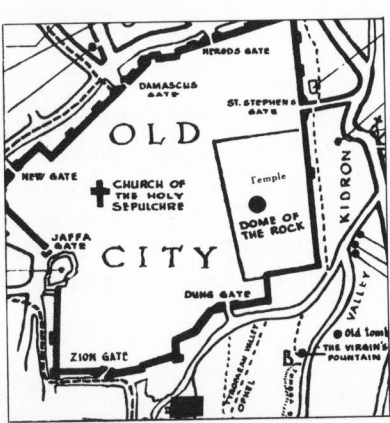

12 — THE POTTER'S FIELD

From the opposite side, we look south across the Hinnom Gorge, where Judas hung himself from the cliff. The property, at that time, was owned by a Potter, but later it was bought from him with the "Thirty Pieces of Silver" —Judas' betrayal money—for a cemetery to bury strangers, thus we have the name, "Potter's Field," to this day. (Matt. 27:9-10.)

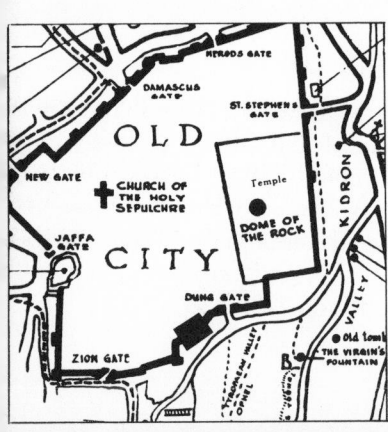

13— CHURCH OF THE VIRGIN

Due north, across Hinnom, is "The Church of the Virgin," on the highest point on Zion. Tradition claims that John's residence once occupied that spot. After Jesus committed his Mother to John's care at "The Cross," she lived with his family over there, the remainder of her days. Caiaphas lived near there, too, and it is fairly certain he was on friendly terms with John. (John 19:25.)

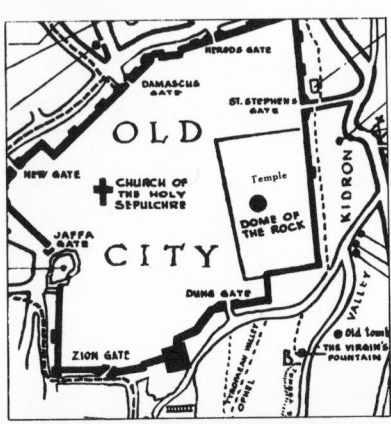

14— HOUSE OF CAIAPHAS

Following a preliminary hearing before Annas, Jesus was brought here to "The House of Caiaphas," the real High Priest, and son-in-law of Annas. After the testimony of some poorly informed witnesses, who perjured themselves, Caiaphas tore his clothes and screamed: "What further need have we for witnesses?" And from here, they took him before the Sanhedrin. (Luke 22:54.)

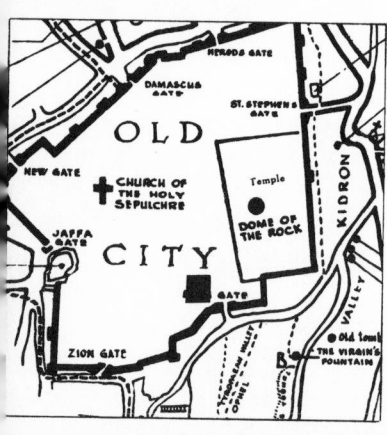

15— ZION FROM MORIAH

The purpose of this picture is to show the distance Jesus was taken from the House of Caiaphas to the Sanhedrin Court in the Temple, the night he was condemned to death. "The Church of the Virgin," over there, is on Zion, and the Temple stood here where the dome is. (Mark 11:1.)

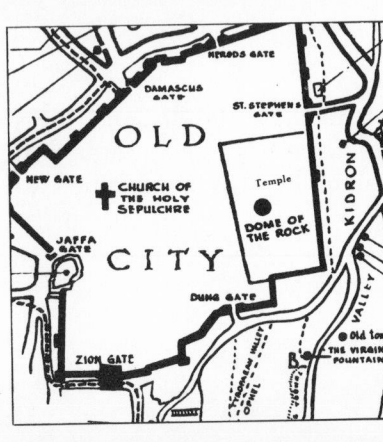

16— ZION GATE

The main entrance to Zion, in those days, was through this Gate. Those arriving from the lower city generally passed through "The Zion Gate" as a short-cut, direct to the Temple, which was on the opposite hill of Moriah, as we have just seen. (Do not neglect the chart.)

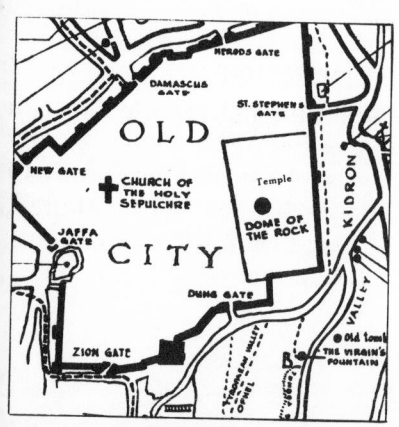

17 — TOMB OF DAVID

Nearby is the "Tomb of David." David wrote about Zion; he sang and prayed about it, and it was his greatest love; so when he died, they buried him on Zion, and this is his Tomb. In Biblical language: "David slept with his fathers, and was buried in the city of David, which is Zion." He reigned over Israel 40 years. (I Kings 2:10.)

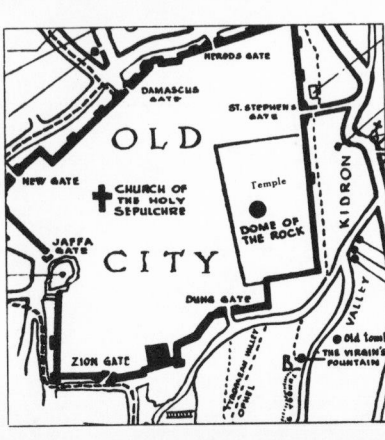

18— THE UPPER ROOM (INTERIOR)

And now, before we leave beautiful and historic Zion, we will step over to the Chapel called "The Upper Room." Here, Jesus, with the Disciples, observed their last Passover together. Here, "The Lord's Supper" was instituted; Jesus washed the Disciples' feet, and finally, "They sang a hymn and went out into the Mount of Olives." (Mark 14:12-26.)

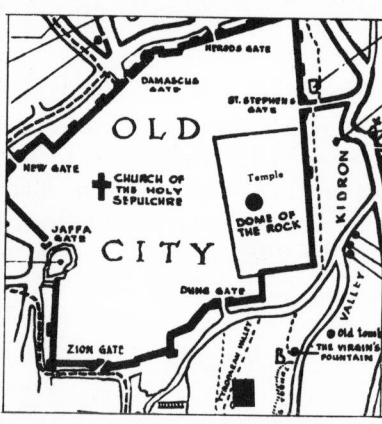

19— JOAB'S WELL

When King David left Jerusalem to escape Absalom, Hushai undertook to delay the King's son from pursuing him, by pretending to be on Absalom's side. The hiding place of Hushai's spies was discovered by a lad, who reported them as being in En Rogel, and while the boy went to report his discovery, they found another hiding place—"Joab's Well." (II Samuel 17:17-22.)

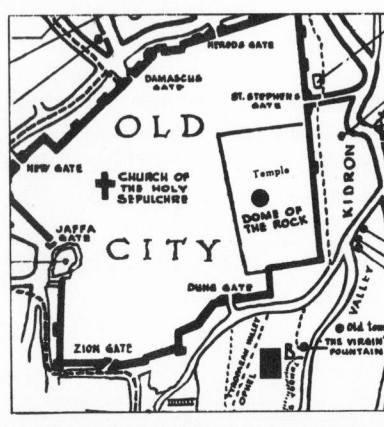

20— POOL OF SILOAM
On the hillside above En Rogel is "The Pool of Siloam." It is an artificial pool which is fed through an aqueduct from "The Virgin's Fountain" farther up the Kedron. After Jesus anointed the eyes of a blind man, on the Mount of Olives, he came to this "Pool of Siloam" and washed, as Jesus directed, and received his sight. (John 9:1.)

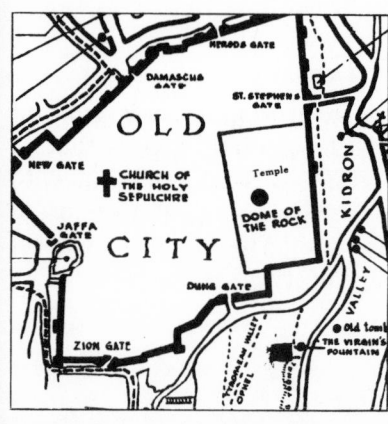

21— HILL OPHEL

This terraced hillside is Ophel. The Ark of the Covenant was first brought here by David, where it remained until the Temple was built on the Hill. "The Mount of Olives" is the highest spot before us and "The Garden of Gethsemane" is up there at its base. Now we will move around the foot of the hill and get a closer view of "The Garden."

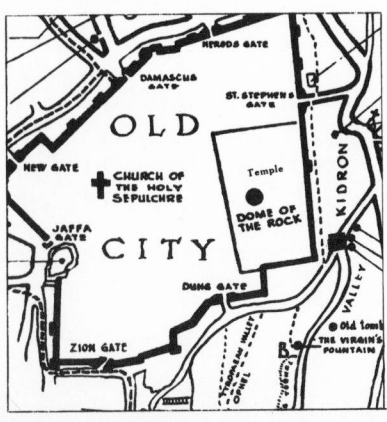

22— OLIVET AND JEHOSHAPHAT

For centuries, Jews have preferred to bury their dead on this hillside. The tomb, with the pyramid top, is that of Zacharias; the one with columns, is Saint James', and to the left is "Absalom's Pillar." The clump of trees is in "The Garden of Gethsemane" and "The Mount of Olives" rises above it. We are looking up the Kedron Valley.

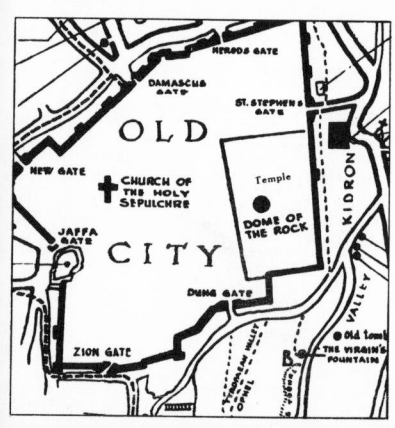

23— THE KEDRON, LOOKING SOUTH (AIR)

We have just been looking up this Valley from underneath the corner of the city wall, and now we are looking down the Kedron (Jehosaphat), from the air. Number 6 is Gethsemane. Stephen was stoned at the curve in the road. Number 3 is Zion; 5, "The Holy Sepulchre," and 4 is "Gordon's Calvary." (Consult the chart.)

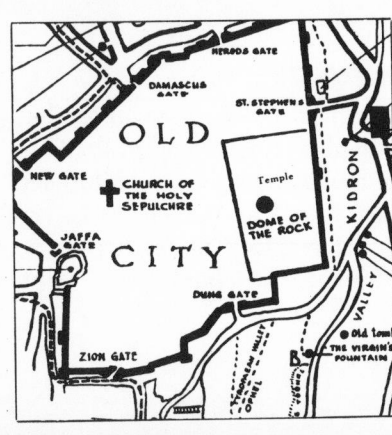

24— GETHSEMANE AND OLIVET

From where we saw the tombs, a moment ago, Jesus came up this little brook and crossed over to "The Garden of Gethsemane," which is in the middle of the picture. The road to the right leads over the hill to Bethany, as does also the one leading straight up the hill before us. (John 18:1.)

25— GARDEN OF GETHSEMANE

Then Jesus, with James, Peter and John, came into the Garden and prayed, while the three slept. The Temple stood behind the wall where you see the dome. The officers, with clanking chains, probably came through the "Golden Gate" over there and crossed the little rivulet lying between, and carried him away in chains. "The Golden Gate" is also the scene of Jesus' "Triumphal Entry." (Matt. 26:36.)

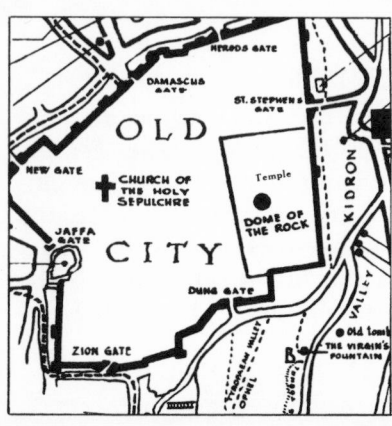

26— THE TREE OF AGONY

This "Tree" is pointed out as the very place where Jesus prayed. If it is not the identical tree, it is believed to be very closely related to it. The betrayer's kiss was given here by Judas, and from here Jesus was cruelly led away, first to Annas, then Caiaphas, next to the Sanhedrin, and finally to Pilot. (Mark 14.)

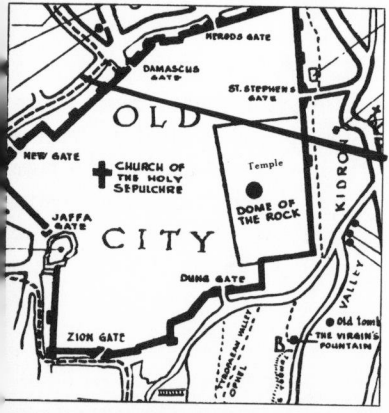

27— JERUSALEM AND OLIVET (FROM THE NORTH)

Lying before us is the entire North Wall, which joins the wall on the east side, down at the corner. Number 2 is the "Museum;" number 3, the Temple enclosure (Mosque of Omar); 4, Church of the Holy Sepulchre. We are looking southeast, and O marks the Mt. of Olives with the Wilderness of Judaea just beyond and the mountains of Moab rising in the distance.

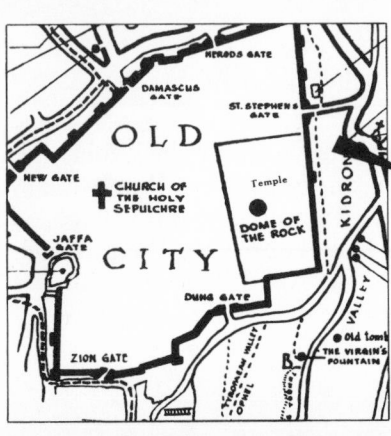

28— SUMMIT OF OLIVET

And here is the Olivet Tower. "And he parted from them and was carried up into Heaven." (Luke 24:51.) "And a cloud received him out of their sight. And behold two men stood by them in white apparel, who said, This Jesus, who was received up from you into Heaven, shall so come in like manner as you beheld him going into Heaven." (Acts 1.)

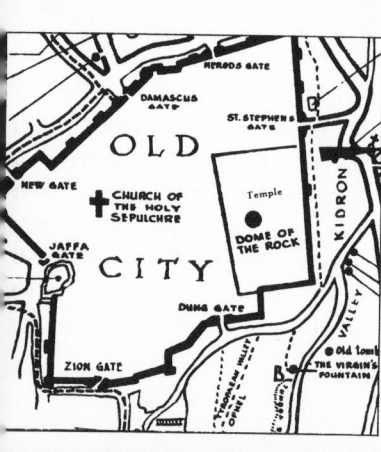

29— CHAPEL OF ASCENSION

So here on the summit of the "Mount of Olives," Jesus commissioned his Disciples to "go into all the world and preach the Gospel," and then ascended up into Heaven. This "Chapel of Ascension" has been erected to commemorate this most sacred event on the spot where it occurred.

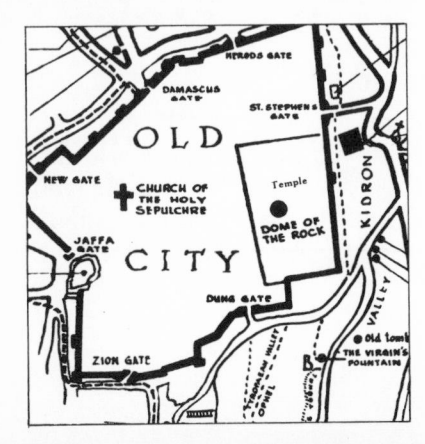

30— JERUSALEM FROM OLIVET

Near this spot, Jesus once sat on dear old Olivet to watch the day die; and we could weep with him as he said, in gentle words: "O Jerusalem, Jerusalem, thou that killest the prophets, and stonest them which are sent unto thee, how often would I have gathered thy children together, even as a hen gathereth her chickens under her wings, and ye would not! Behold, your house is left unto you desolate." (Matt. 23:37-38.)

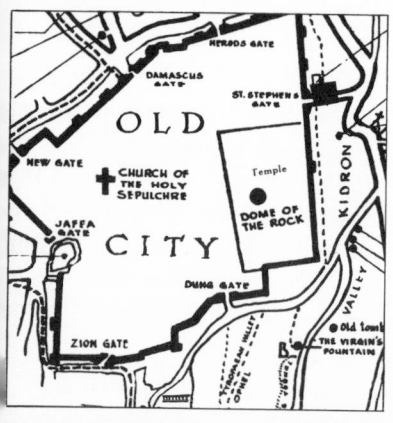

31— SAINT STEPHEN'S GATE

"Saint Stephen's Gate" is a few hundred feet north of "The Golden Gate," in the east wall. In Jesus' day it was called "The Sheep Gate," but after they stoned Stephen, near this point, its name was changed to "Saint Stephen's Gate," the name by which it has been known since that day. (Acts 7:59-60.)

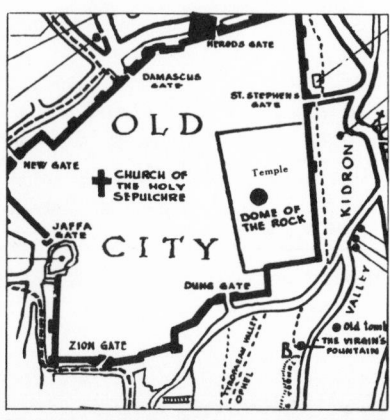

32— NORTH WALL

The north wall of Jerusalem is in the best state of preservation of any other portion, and we pass here because we can see it as it looked in the days when Bible characters lived here. The walls were built, of course, for protective purposes, but it would not stand for a single minute under our modern weapons of destruction.

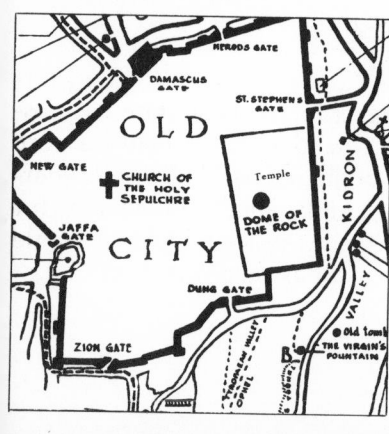

33— DAMASCUS GATE

Near the west end of the wall we have just seen is "The Damascus Gate." Today it is the most frequented and the most beautiful entrance to Jerusalem. All travelers from the north pass through it, and by far the greatest part of the Holy Land lies to the north. We will now climb to the top of the wall and see the knoll called "Gordon's Calvary."

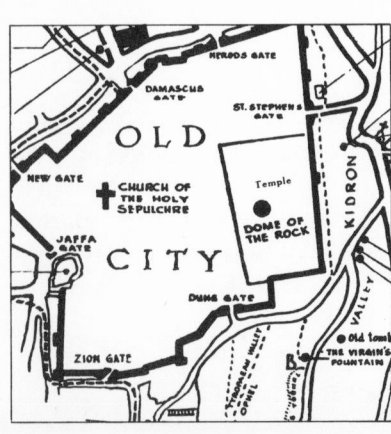

34— GORDON'S CALVARY

Many believe that Jesus was crucified here: first, because it is located outside the walls; second, Golgotha means "place of a skull," and with a little stretch of imagination, you can see, in the base of the hill, some resemblance to a skull; and third, a garden lies at the base, and there are ancient tombs cut out of the solid rock.

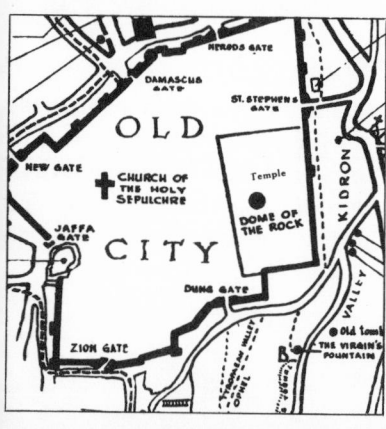

35— THE GARDEN TOMB

And here, at the foot of the cliff, is a tomb. One could easily believe that it was once owned by a wealthy man like Joseph of Arimathaea. In fact, many scholars agree that this hill is the real "Calvary," and that Jesus was buried here. (See the chart.)

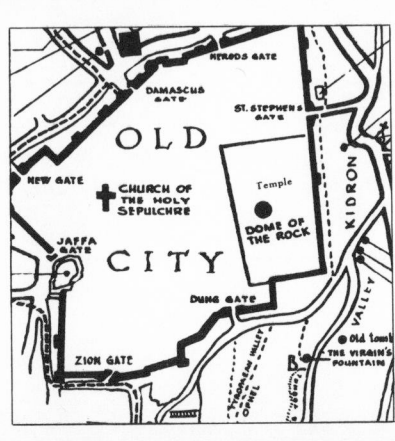

36— TOMB (INTERIOR)

This is the old sarcophagus in the tomb, which also favors the opinion that the grave once belonged to a person of importance. If so, then Joseph of Arimathaea and Nicodemus buried the Master here and on the third day He arose, as he had promised, and when the Marys came to the tomb, early Easter morning, he was not there.

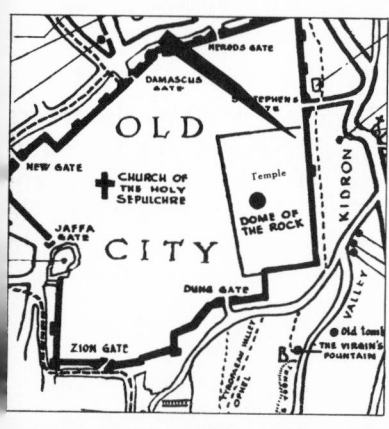

37— FROM GORDON'S CALVARY

We are standing on Gordon's Calvary and below us is the garden. Farther on is the picturesque wall we have just seen, while beyond, in the distance, is the Tower on the Mount of Olives, from where Jesus "ascended," and where we stood a moment ago.

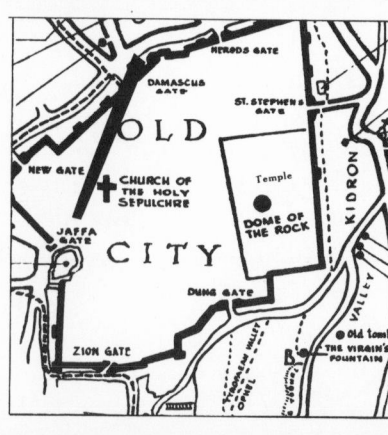

38— JERUSALEM FROM GORDON'S CALVARY

Before we leave "Gordon's Calvary," let us look over the walls. The distant tower is "The Church of the Virgin" on Mount Zion. The square building is the "Tower of David" at the "Joppa Gate," and the dome is "The Church of the Holy Sepulchre," which stands far inside the north wall, where we shall go presently.

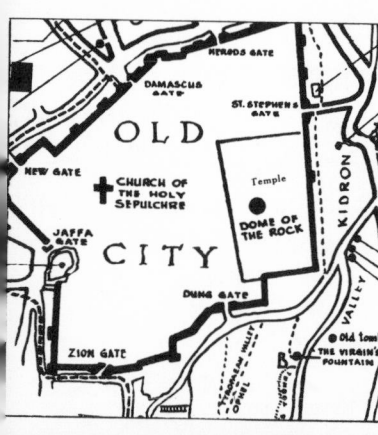

39— THE Y.M.C.A.

Jerusalem also has a modern Y.M.C.A. It was donated to Jerusalem by a Christian gentleman who wished to do something in the name of Jesus, for all the people. But it so happens, when the division was made between the two quarrelsome boys of Abraham, it was found to be on the Jewish side of the barbed-wire entanglement, not far from the "Joppa Gate."

40— DAVID STREET (LOOKING EAST)

Passing through "The Joppa Gate" we enter "David Street" to face a motley group like this. Before the big fuss began, you could find the principal shops, tourist agencies, banks, etc., in this neighborhood. But most of these, now, are beyond the barbed-wire entanglement, and this spot is practically deserted. (Note black square on chart.)

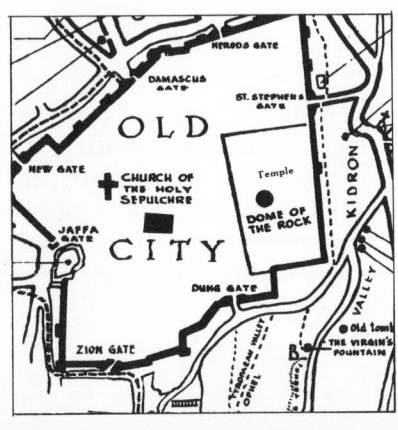

41– DAVID STREET (LOOKING WEST)

Here we make a complete about face. To our right is the old "Grand Hotel;" to the left, is the corner of "David's Tower" and straight ahead is the opening where the wall was torn out for Kaiser William's "triumphal entry" into Jerusalem, which lasted about a minute. On the right of the opening, is the inside of "The Joppa Gate." The ancient moat protected "David's Tower."

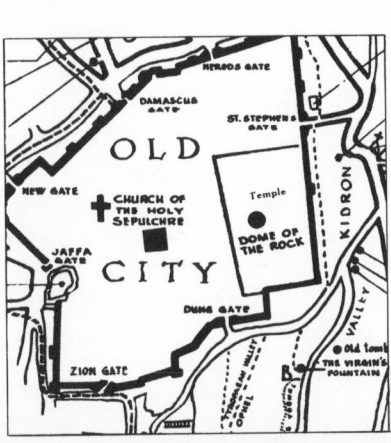

42— DARK STREET

What you saw in the last picture is not all of "David Street." It continues through narrow, dark passages, from there to "Saint Stephen's Gate" on the opposite side of the city, and passes "The Ecce Homo Arch" and "The Antonia."

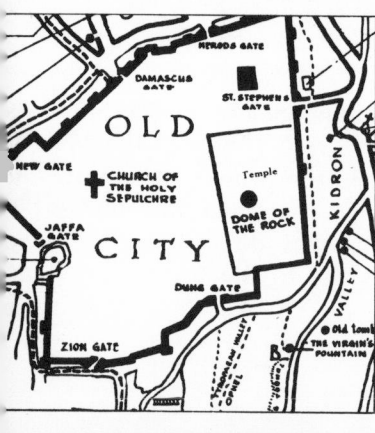

43– POOL OF BETHESDA

En route to Moriah, we pass "The Pool of Bethesda," which, at one time, was surrounded by five porches, with its crowds of people stricken with all manner of diseases, waiting to be healed by plunging into its troubled waters. One day, Jesus, while mingling with the gruesome crowd, healed an impotent man who had been waiting for 38 years to get into the pool. (John 9:1.)

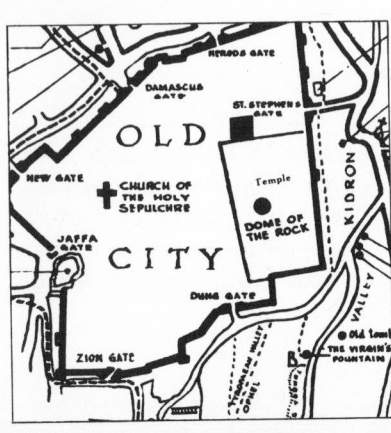

44— ECCE HOMO ARCH

At the north end of the Temple enclosure (Moriah), we pass under this "Ecce Homo Arch" ("Behold the Man"). When Pilot presented Jesus to the people, those were his words. At one time, this arch was apparently inside the building, and Pilate's throne was directly under it. So when he gave out any message to the people, he stood at this point. (John 19:5.)

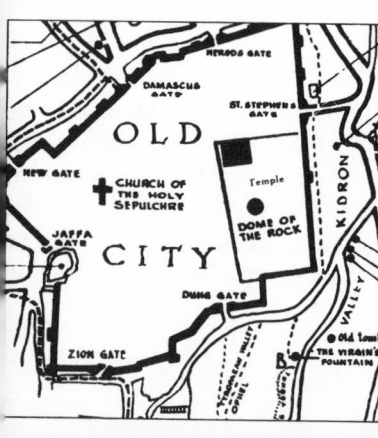

45— TOWER OF ANTONIA

A portion of the same building, connected with the last picture, is "The Tower of Antonia." In Pilate's day, the capital was Caesarea, but when he came to Jerusalem he used this as his Government house. Jesus was brought before Pilate here from the Sanhedrin Court, which is back of us. All the rest of "The Trial" was conducted here.

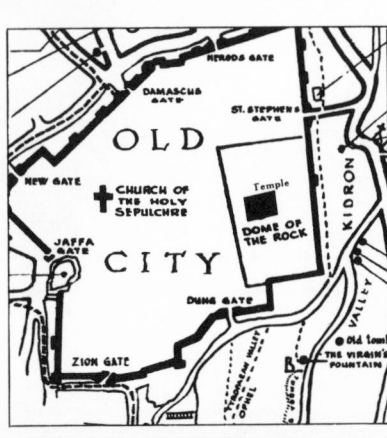

46— TEMPLE AREA (LOOKING NORTH — AIR)

"The Antonia" stands in the upper left corner of the enclosure. From the right side, the precipitous cliff drops abruptly into the Valley of Jehoshaphat, and "Gethsemane" is just to the right of it. The depression on the left is "The Tyropean Valley," and a bridge crossed the ravine, from the Temple to the main city, in Solomon's day.

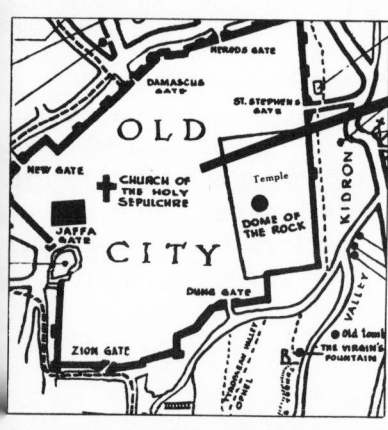

47– MORIAH AND OLIVET

Here is the Temple enclosure and Olivet, as seen from "David's Tower" near the "Joppa Gate." So we trust that with this effort to locate the position of the Temple, you have it thoroughly in mind and will be ready to appreciate it with all of its surroundings.

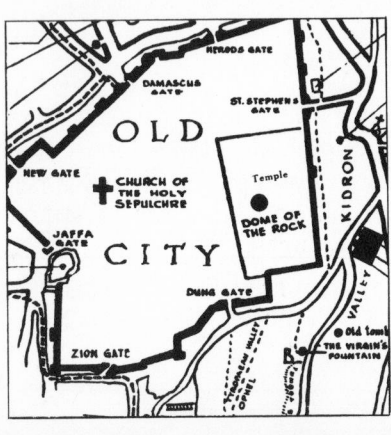

48— THE TEMPLE FROM OLIVET

Here we are, standing on the southern end of the Mount of Olives, and this deep gorge is "The Valley of Jehoshaphat." When the Temple was destroyed, much of the rubbish was dumped into this valley. But a great deal of it was finally salvaged and built into Bethlehem's Nativity, "The Holy Sepulchre," and "The Mosque of Omar."

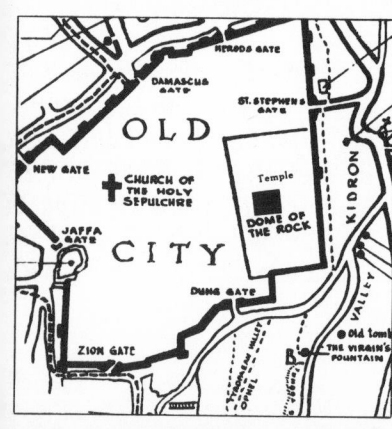

49— TEMPLE ENCLOSURE

Here, then, is where Solomon's Temple once stood. This is "The Mosque of Omar" (or, "Dome of the Rock"), "The Mosque of Alaksa" to the right (distance). This hill (Moriah), was once a threshing floor. David purchased it from Araunah (2 Sam. 24:18), but God would not permit David to build the Temple because he was too much given to war, so it was left for Solomon to build.

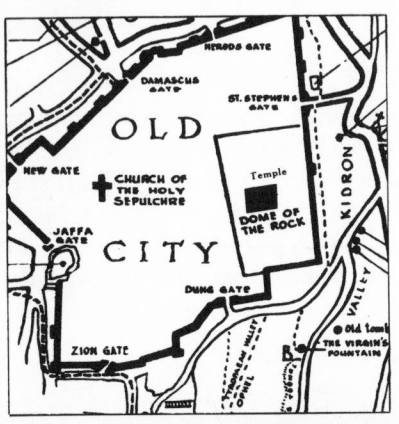

50— MOSQUE OF OMAR OR DOME OF THE ROCK

"The Mosque of Omar" on Mt. Moriah, is one of the world's most beautiful buildings. It is octagonal and each panel is 66 feet long. The diameter is 174 feet, with an 87 foot dome. And the height of the entire building is 108 feet. It is also called "The Dome of the Rock," and its history dates back to Abraham. (Note chart with every picture.)

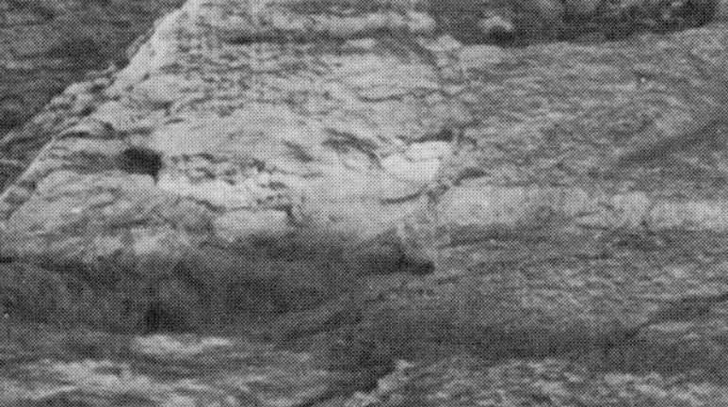

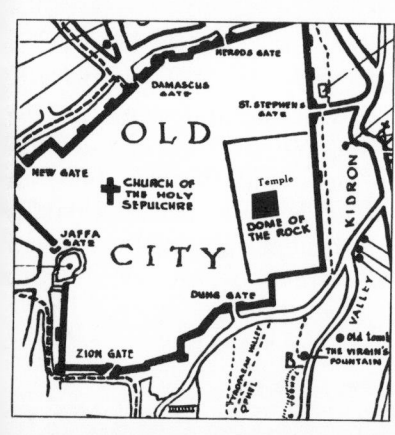

51— MOSQUE OF OMAR (INTERIOR)

Pushing itself up through the floor is the rock upon which Abraham built an altar to sacrifice his son, Isaac. This particular stone was directly in front of the entrance to Solomon's Temple and his Altar of Burnt-offering stood on it. The columns you see were salvaged from the rubbish in the Valley of Jehoshaphat just mentioned. (Gen. 22.)

52— THE ROCK

From the Dome, we are looking straight down on the Rock. It is suggested that the hole in it was the channel that carried the blood of the sacrifices away into the Valley below. Directly under this Rock are the Quarries of Solomon. The Rock, when beaten upon, gives a sort of hollow sound, and the superstitious like to tell you that it is miraculously suspended beneath the "sacred" Dome

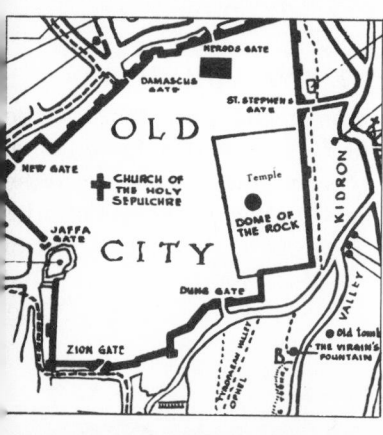

53— SOLOMON'S QUARRIES (INTERIOR)

"Solomon's Quarries" lie far below the surface of Jerusalem. Sidonians cut the stones from these very walls and placed them in the Temple for Solomon. Unfinished stones are seen with chisel marks as fresh as though the masons left them but yesterday. These cut stones were evidently lifted up through some cavity made in the ceiling, but such an opening has never been satisfactorily located.

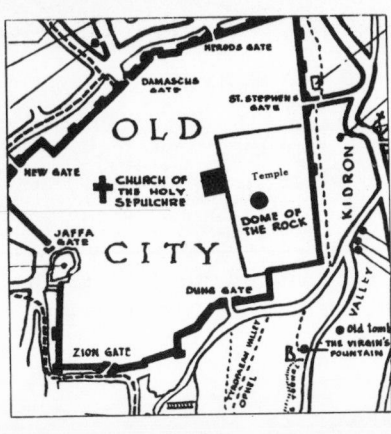

54— WORSHIPPERS AT THE "WAILING WALL'

Here are some of the very stones that were taken from the Quarry; all that is left of the original Temple. It is called "The Wailing Wall." Devout Jews once came here every Friday to pray for the restoration of the Temple to them, but up to now God has not done it, and today they are entirely shut off from this holy place.

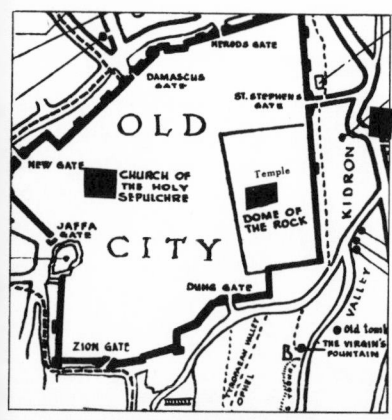

55— HOLY SEPULCHRE AND MORIAH

The rest of our stay in Jerusalem will be devoted to "The Church of the Holy Sepulchre," where tradition places "The Crucifixion" of our Lord. Pilate surrendered Jesus to be crucified, in his court, near the Temple (at the small dome). He was driven from that point to Calvary, the large dome—the distance was something less than a mile.

(Locate on chart—black square.)

56— HOLY SEPULCHRE (AIR)

"The Church of the Holy Sepulchre" is down where you see the two domes. We will call one "The Large Dome" and the other "The Small Dome." Here you will see how it is environed. Over where you see the black portion (shrubs), is the north wall of the city, and "Gordon's Calvary." So next we will land and get a close view of the church. (Locate on chart—black square.)

57—ENTRANCE TO THE CHURCH

In this picture you have the main entrance and the Small Dome. This dome is built over what is believed to have been "Calvary," or "Golgotha." You can see the beginning of the curve of the "Large Dome" behind "The Tower" and that "Large Dome" covers Jesus' Tomb. Now we will step inside the entrance, here under the "Small Dome."

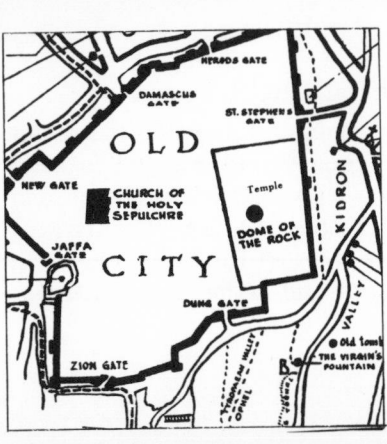

58— CHURCH INTERIOR — UNDER SMALL DOME

This altar stands directly under the "Small Dome" and marks the spot where "The Cross" stood. Many interesting features, indicating that this is the very place of "Crucifixion," are shown; even the cleft in the rock, which was caused by the earthquake, when the sun faded from sight and Jesus died on Calvary. (Matt. 27.)

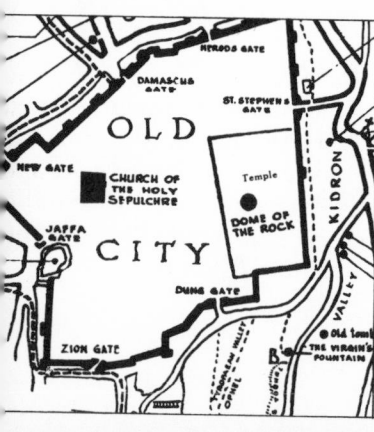

59— CHURCH INTERIOR

In the same Chapel, only a few feet from the altar we have just seen, is another altar located in this beautiful wing in the building. Here, we are told, our Lord was stripped of his robes and then nailed to "The Cross," while the mob jeered and mocked. There was no building here, of course, when "The Crucifixion" occurred.

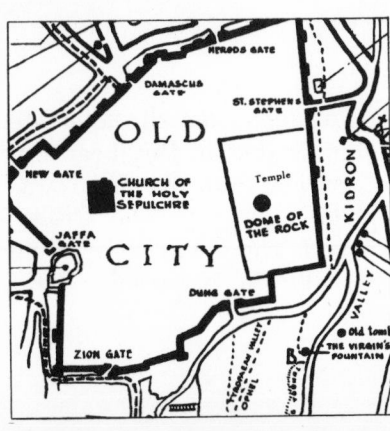

60— LARGE DOME

And now let us move outside the church again and see the majestic dome which covers the burial place of our Lord. His was a "borrowed" tomb, and its owner was one Joseph of Arimathaea. This is the most revered spot in the entire Holy Land. Now we will move through the entrance and see the richly decorated interior.

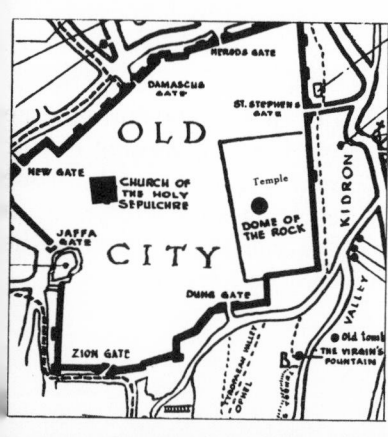

61— THE HOLY SEPULCHRE

Upon entering the church, we find ourselves directly under the "Large Dome" which covers the Tomb of Jesus. It is decorated with golden lamps and candlesticks that are kept burning day and night. It presents a picture never to be forgotten. You will notice the pedestal inside the door.

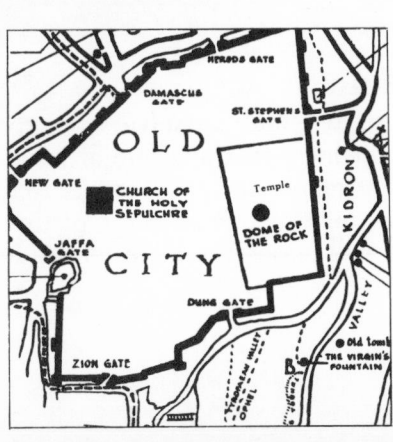

62– THE GRAVE STONE

We are now past the door, and are inside the canopy, and here, on the pedestal, is a stone in the form of a disc, with which the "Grave of Jesus" was closed. This kind of door is very common in Palestine, or once was, and may still be seen in many cemeteries.

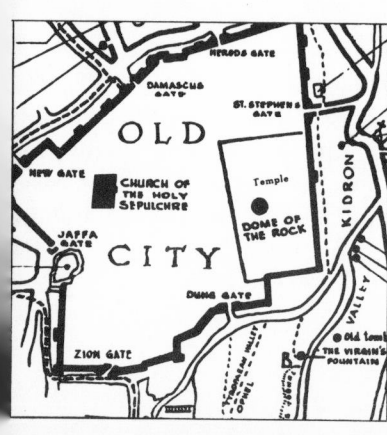

63— THE TOMB

This is "The Tomb" itself, where Jesus lay until his "Resurrection." Here, then, the kindly hands of Joseph and Nicodemus laid his body to rest, and in this very spot an angel announced to the bewildered women on that first Easter morning: "He is not here; for He is risen, as He said." (Matt. 28.)

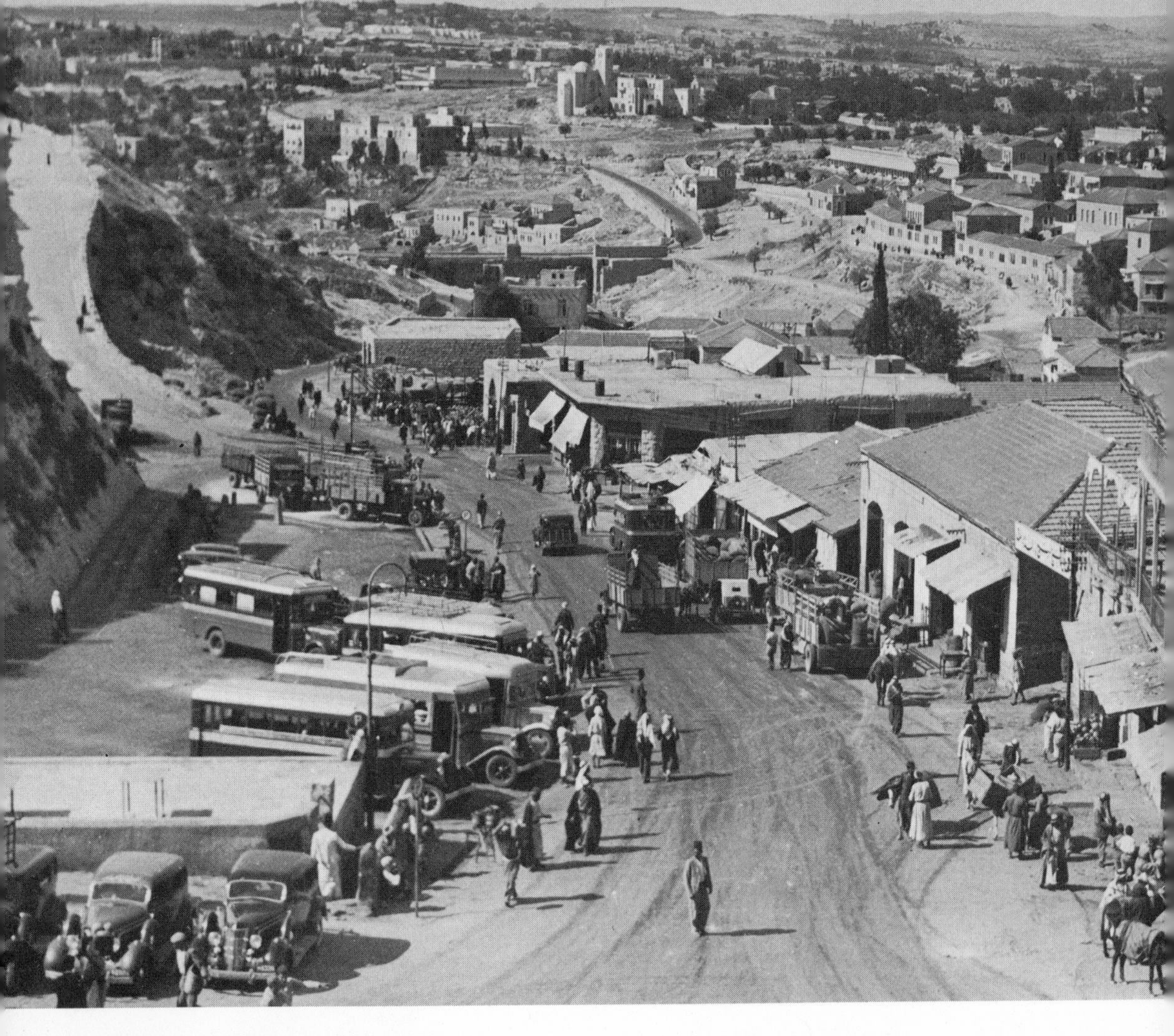

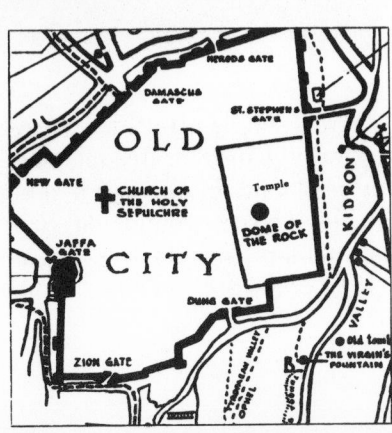

64— ROAD TO BETHLEHEM

The "Joppa Gate" is behind us, "Zion" is to the left, the undulating plain is Rephaim, and we are now taking our leave of the Holy City, facing the south. Abraham traveled that road to Hebron and Beersheba, David fought his last battle on Rephaim (2 Sam. 5), and "The Wise Men" followed this road to the crib of "The Holy Babe of Bethlehem."

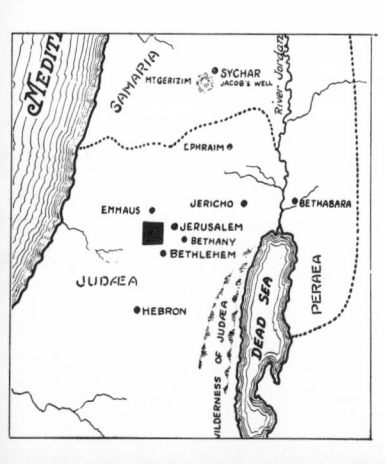

65— RACHEL'S TOMB

On Jacob's return trip from Padan-Aram with his wives, concubines, and eleven children, his wife, Rachel, gave birth to Benjamin at Ephrath, which is near Bethlehem, and died. Jacob buried her here by the roadside, and placed a marker on her grave, which is the first memorial erected to the dead, mentioned in the Bible. (Gen. 35:16.)

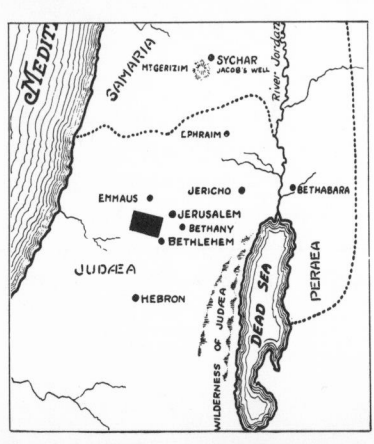

66— APPROACH TO BETHLEHEM

Just beyond, and in sight of Rachel's Tomb, is Bethlehem. As we raise our eyes from the last scene, these passers-by attract our attention. They are going up there to Bethlehem, over the same road that was traveled by "The Wise Men from the East" nearly 2,000 years ago, seeking him who was born "King of the Jews." (Matt. 2:2.)

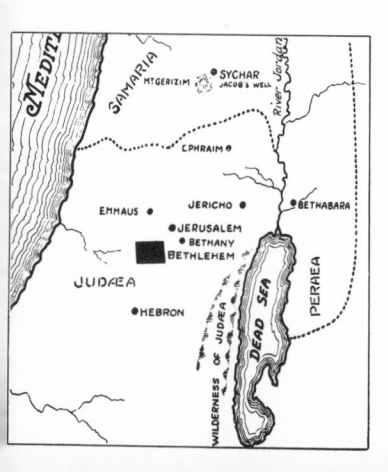

67— BETHLEHEM

Another moment brings us into full view of the city, and our thoughts almost bewilder us, as the names of Ruth, Naomi, Boaz, Joab, David, and the Baby Jesus flood our minds. But, of course, many scenes in the Holy Lands bring similar mental reactions, as Nazareth, Capernaum, or Calvary, all of which we are to visit, and hundreds more. (The map on every page is your guide. Keep your eye on the black square.)

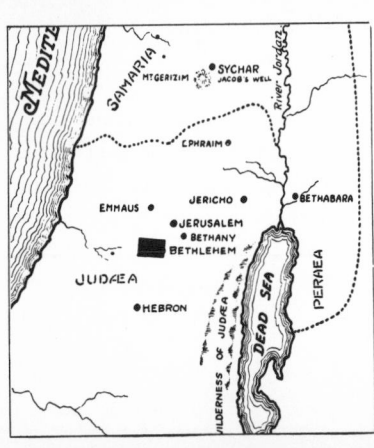

68— FIELD OF BOAZ

This field once belonged to Boaz, who met a girl, a gleaner, (Ruth), and fell in love with her and they were married, and the names of some of their posterity are David, Solomon, and Jesus. One day, in this very field the shepherd boy, David, was visited by the great Prophet Samuel, who anointed him King of Israel, to succeed Saul. (I Sam. 16:16-18.)

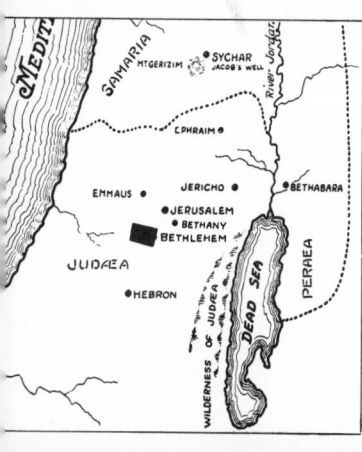

69— THE SHEPHERD'S FIELD

Now it is called "The Shepherd's Field," and one night, "There were shepherds in the same country, abiding in the field, and keeping watch over their flock," when an angel appeared to them and said: "I bring you good tidings of great joy, for there is born unto you, in the city of David, a Savior, who is Christ the Lord," etc. (Luke 2:8-16.)

70— CHURCH OF THE NATIVITY

There was only a little cave in the hillside here, used to shelter animals, when the shepherds arrived from "The Shepherd's Field" and found Jesus lying in "The Manger." Queen Helena, mother of the emperor, Constantine, built this magnificent basilica over the place, and the story of Jesus has been heralded from here ever since that day.

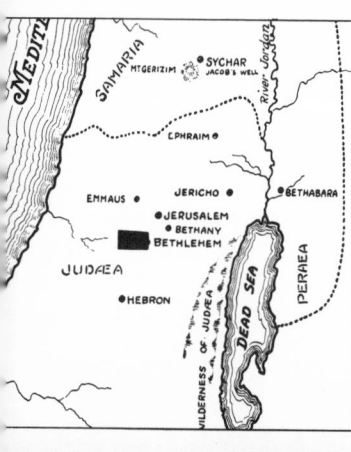

71— CHURCH OF NATIVITY (INTERIOR)

The interior of the Nativity is attractive, but the source of the material built into it enhances its real value to all who lend a sentimental value to rare things. All these beautiful columns and capitols, as previously mentioned, were salvaged from the rubbish of the Temple in Jerusalem, by Queen Helena, and built into this wonderful structure.

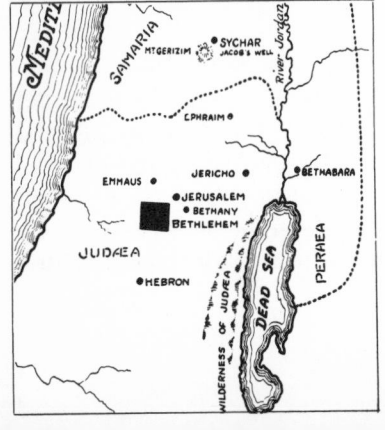

72— THE GROTTO OF NATIVITY

Underneath the shelves of rock that were one time so un-inviting, we now see a beautifully decorated altar, sur-sounded by a wilderness of beautiful gold and silver chan-deliers and candlesticks that are kept lighted perpetually. Beneath the altar is a solid silver star which is said to occupy the exact spot where Jesus was born. But now we leave Bethlehem and resume our journey to the south.

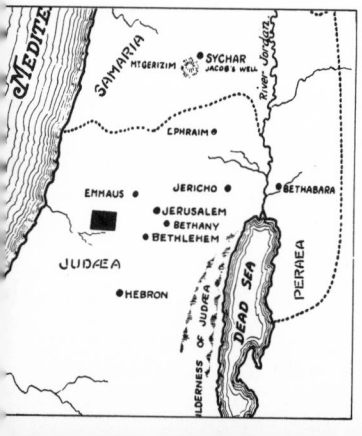

73— THE VALLEY OF ELAH

In the days of King Saul, when David was a boy, the Philistine army was encamped at Shocho, over on that hill, some ten miles from Bethlehem. Here David met the giant, Goliath, and without arms or armor, except a little sling, slew the human monster down there by the Brook Elah, with the first twirling of his sling. Then he decapitated him with the giant's own sword. (I Sam. 17.)

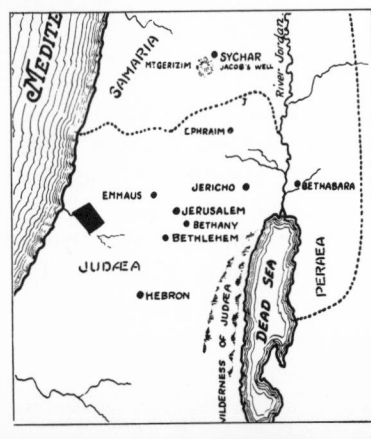

74— THE COUNTRY OF GATH

The Philistine's champion slain, they fled in confusion down this valley to their capital, Gath. Many were so frightened that they ran past their city without recognizing it. But strange to say, long after this, Achish, King of Gath, saved David's life, and finally made him ruler of Ziklag. (I Samuel 5:2; 21:10.)

75— GAZA

Another of the five great Philistine cities was Gaza, near the sea, and Samson and Delilah once lived here. The deceit and unfaithfulness of Delilah resulted in a prison sentence for her husband, who was also blinded, mocked and maltreated by the Philistines. He finally pulled down "The Temple of Dagon" over the heads of 5,000 banquetors, which destroyed both the merrymakers and himself. (Judges 16:3.) Gaza is the center of contention between the Arab and Jew today, 1957-1958.

76— GERAR

Gerar, a beautiful community on a perennial streamlet like this, but with a forgotten identity, was ruled by Abimelech, in the days of Abraham. Here, again, he denied that Sarah was his wife, and Abimelech was at the verge of adding her to his harem when he awakened to the fact that Abraham was not telling the truth. Isaac was born here when Abraham was 100. (Gen. 20:1.

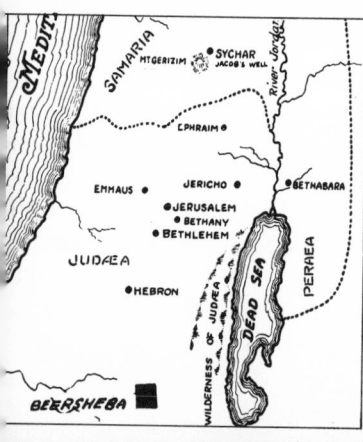

77— "THE WELL OF THE OATH"

Abimelech then expelled both of them from Gerar. Abraham moved down the valley of the little streamlet and Abimelech made him a visit, and they dug a well and swore by it that they would live peaceably, by having little to do with each other. The meaning of Beersheba is "Well of the Oath," and this is the well. (Gen. 21.) Later, Isaac had a similar experience at this same well.

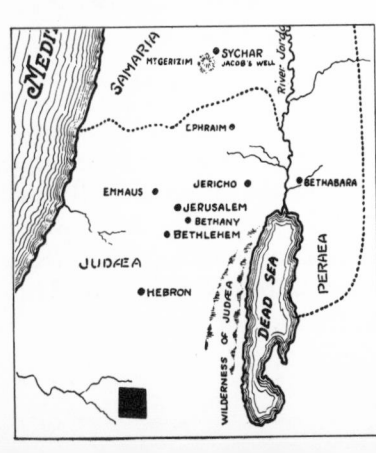

78— BEERSHEBA

Beersheba has been a crossroads from all directions for all time, a kind of "Division Point." Hagar's son, Ishmael, was sent out from here by his father, Abraham. (Gen. 21.) Today the most bitter groups in the world toward each other are the offspring of Isaac (Jews) and the offspring of Ishmael (Arabs). Sinai lies further south, but we will visit that later, and now return northward.

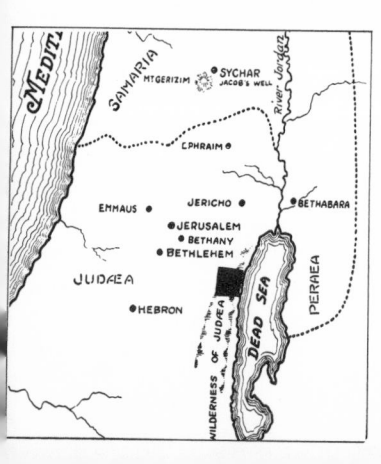

79— CLIFFS OF ENGIDI

While Saul was in pursuit of David, he remained among the "Cliffs of Engidi" and one night, while the king slept, David cut off the skirt of his cloak and then taunted him from across the canyon. David had Saul's life in his hand but did not take advantage of it. So Saul gathered his army together and went home, admitting he had been outwitted by David. (I Sam. 23.)

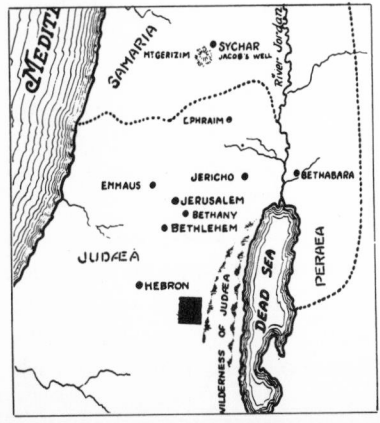

80– CARMEL IN JUDAH

Nabal, wealthy land owner, husband of Abigail, and a drunkard, lived here at Carmel, and was protected by David's army, but refused to share supplies with him. So Abigail called on David, who was at the point of taking what he needed by force. When she told Nabal, it so frightened him that he fell dead, and David married his widow. (I Sam. 25.) Abiather met young David (I Sam. 22), and Jonathan swore eternal friendship to David at Ziph, near here. (I Sam. 23.)

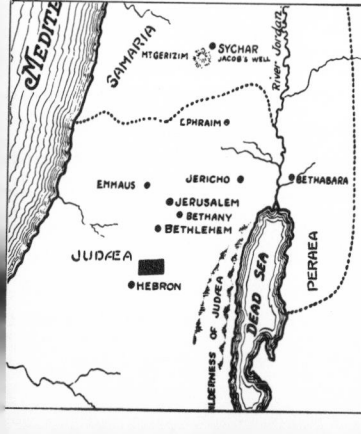

81— THE ANCIENT OAK OF MAMRE

After Abraham and Lot separated, Abraham pitched his tent here among the "Oaks of Mamre." (Gen. 13:18.) He was informed at that time that he would have another son by Sarah, whose age was 90. The historic oaks of Mamre are about extinct. In fact, there is but one of this venerable family of trees in the world, and "it has seen its best days." However, it is being humored and cared for in every way known by the tree surgeon. Its health is much improved and it appears now that it may be with us for quite some time.

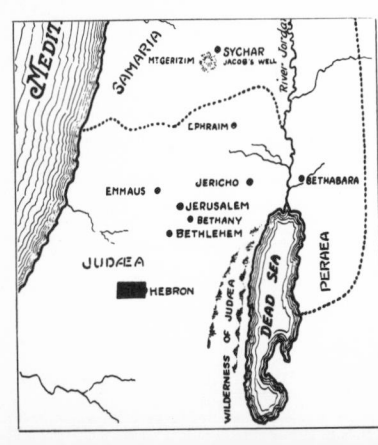

82— HEBRON

Hebron lies three miles down the Valley of Eschol from Mamre. It is the oldest city in the world, and has a great history. Abraham, Isaac and Jacob lived here. Joseph was sent from here to Dothan, where he was sold by his brothers. David was crowned King of Judah (2 Sam. 2: 3-4), and Absalom's rebellion started here. The large building (left) is Machpelah.

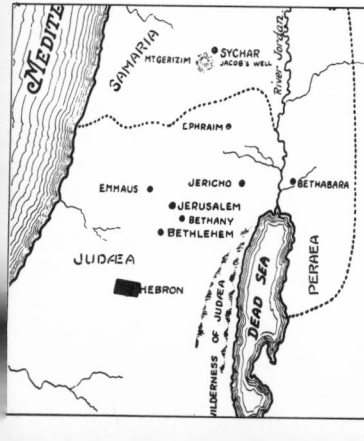

83— MOSQUE OF MACHPELAH

When Sarah died in Hebron, Abraham bought "The Cave of Machpelah" for 400 shekels of silver as a burial place for his wife. Finally, Abraham, Isaac and Jacob were also buried here. And when the Moslems took over, they built this great mosque, and it is one of the most sacred spots in the Moslem world. (Gen. 23.)

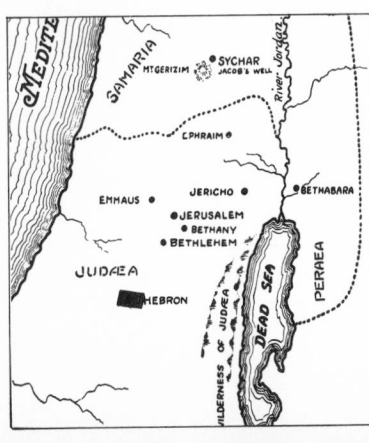

84– POOL OF HEBRON

After the death of Saul at Gilboa, David had but one rival for the throne–Ishbasheth–the imbecile son of Saul. The son was murdered at Mahanaim, and his head was brought here to David by Baanali and Rachab. David was deeply distressed and had the two men "hanged over the Pool of Hebron." (2 Sam. 4.) Joab also slew Abner here. (2 Sam. 2.)

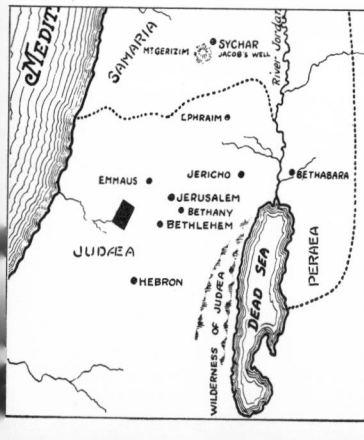

85— AIN KARIM

Five miles west of Jerusalem, in the "hill country of Judaea," lies Ain Karim, home of Zacharias and Elizabeth, parents of John the Baptist, who was born here. Following "The Annunciation" at Nazareth, the Virgin Mary visited her cousin Elizabeth here and remained with them several months. The church is dedicated to John the Baptist.

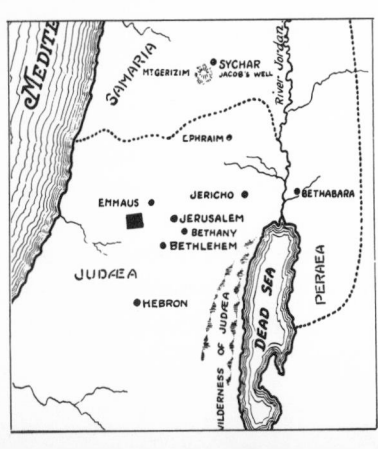

86— KIRJATH-JEARIM

Some five miles further we pass the village of Kirjath-Jearim. The captured "Ark of the Covenant" was stored here for 20 years after it had wrought havoc at Ashdod, Gath and Bethshemish. When David became king, he brought it from here to the "Hill Ophel" (Jerusalem), where it remained until Solomon completed the Temple. (I Sam. 7.) (Don't neglect the map on every page.)

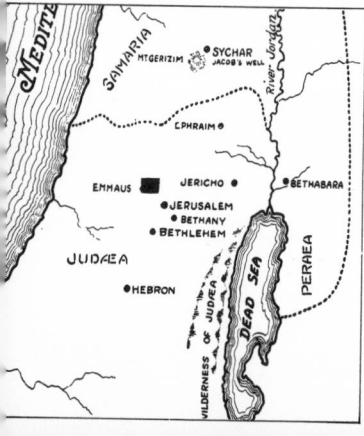

87— EMMAUS

This is Emmaus, six miles west of Jerusalem. The same day Jesus arose from the dead, two men were returning to their home here, and Jesus overtook them, but they did not recognize him. They invited him into their home and while they were dining, he revealed himself to them. Then Jesus slipped away and appeared to them all later in the evening, in the "Upper Room" in Jerusalem. (Luke 24:13.)

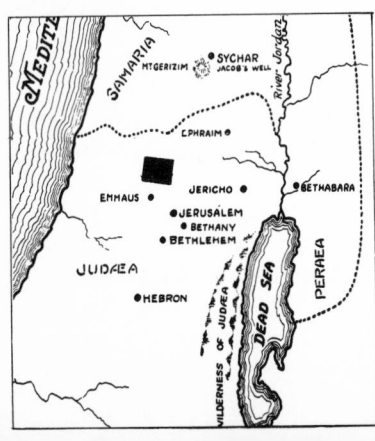

88— RAMAH

Ramah, birthplace of Samuel, is five miles north of Jerusalem. His mother, Hannah, promised, before he was born, that she would dedicate him to the Lord. So, after Samuel was weaned, he was left with Eli, the High Priest at Shiloh, and later became a great Prophet. (I Sam. 1.) When Nebuchadnezzar took Jerusalem, his prisoners were guarded here and among them was Jeremiah. (Jer. 40.)

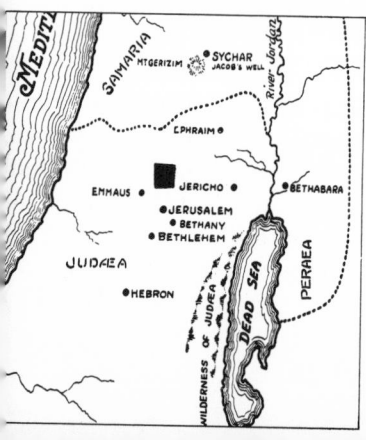

89— GIBEON

When Joshua got to Shechem, the people of Gibeon sent a committee to seek his protection from the fate he had meted out to Ai and Jericho, and Joshua made a covenant with them. (Joshua 9:3.) It was also at Gibeon that God promised Solomon He would give him anything that he might ask, and the king asked for "wisdom" and got it. Abishai, Joab's brother, was slain here by Abner. (2 Sam. 2.)

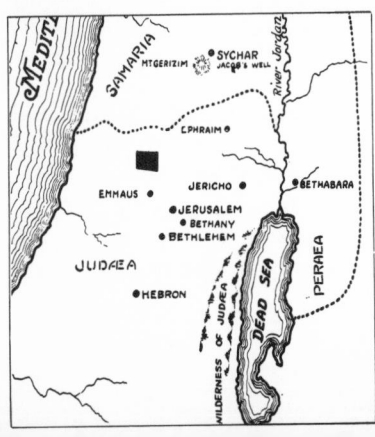

90— BETH-HORON

Soon after this covenant with Joshua, Gibeon was attacked by five kings of the south, and Joshua, true to his promise, came to their rescue here at Beth-Horon. While the battle raged, a downpour of rocks was rained from heaven on the enemy and destroyed the greater part of them. The five kings were captured and later put to death. (Joshua 16.)

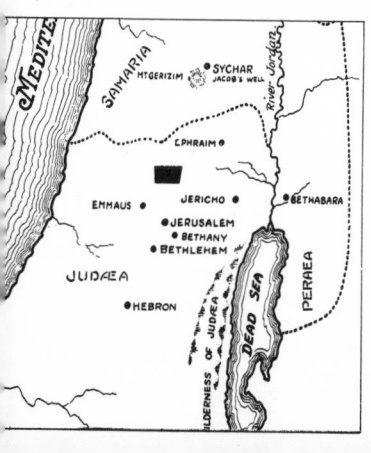

91— AJALON

The remnant of the army of the five kings was pursued here to the Valley of Ajalon, where the battle continued until late in the evening when Joshua commanded: "Sun, stand thou still upon Gibeon; and thou, moon, in the Valley of Ajalon." The sun stood still, and the moon stayed, until the people had avenged themselves upon their enemies. (Joshua 10:12-13.)

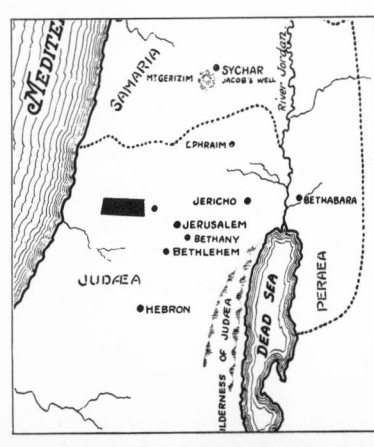

92— ZORAH

Atop this hill, overlooking the Plain of Sharon, about 10 miles from Jerusalem, is Zorah, birthplace of Samson. (Judges 13:2.) When he pulled down the Temple of Dagon on the 5,000 lords at Gaza, he was also crushed to death by the falling Temple. His brothers buried him here at Zorah, and this is his tomb. (Judges 16:31.)

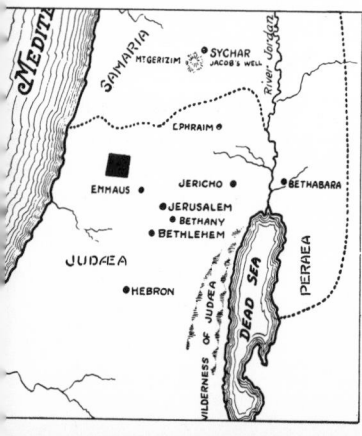

93— THE WHEAT FIELD

From the foot of the mountain at Zorah, the Plain of
Sharon spreads out to the north and west, like this, and
Timnath was located in the midst of a great grain field.
Samson's marriage at Timnath ended in a terrible tragedy.
The Philistines captured his wife and father-in-law and
burned them to death, and Samson retaliated by burning
their grain fields. (Judges 14.)

94— VALLEY OF SOREK

We have just left those hills—Zorah. The valley below is Sorek, the ruin here is Bethshemish, and Timnath is down the valley. One day Samson was attacked by a lion down there by the brook, and he slew the beast with his bare hands. (Judges 14:5-6.) Farther up this valley (east), the boy David slew the giant, Goliath, many years after this incident. We are now 13 miles west of Jerusalem.

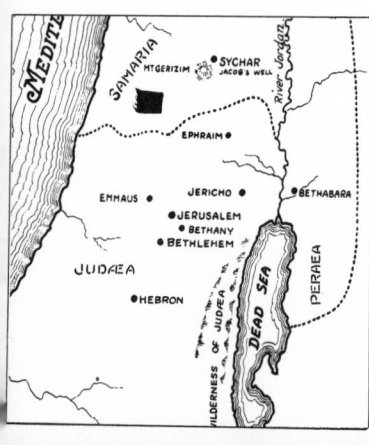

95— ANTIPATRIS

Now before we move over to Joppa, we will digress a short way northward over the Plain of Sharon to this little streamlet, where in Jesus' day, stood the Village of Antipatris. To avoid a Jewish uprising against Paul in Jerusalem, he was taken to Caesarea for trial and remained at Antipatris over night. (Acts 23:31.)

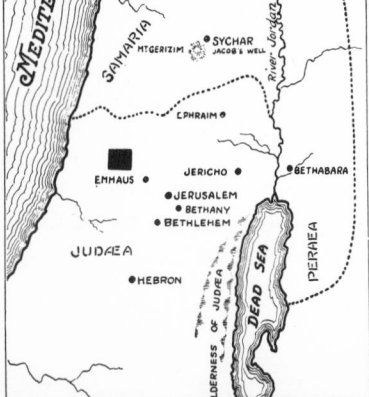

96— EMWAS

A short distance west, on our way to Joppa, is Emwas. When Jesus was crucified, he hung between two convicted thieves. To one, Jesus said: "This day shall thou be with me in Paradise." There is a very ancient tradition stating that both of these thieves lived here in Emwas. The original Trapist Monastery is located here, and it is conducted with the most severe discipline.

97— LYDDA

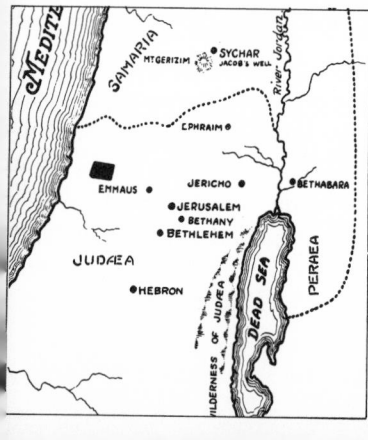

In the heart of the Plain of Sharon stands this very ancient town of Lydda. Peter, while on one of his missionary journeys, called on Aeneas, who had been sick for eight years, and healed him. (Acts 10:32-35.) Then he was called from here to Joppa, where he restored Dorcas to life, as we shall see later. One minister of the early church at Lydda was Saint George, Patron Saint of England.

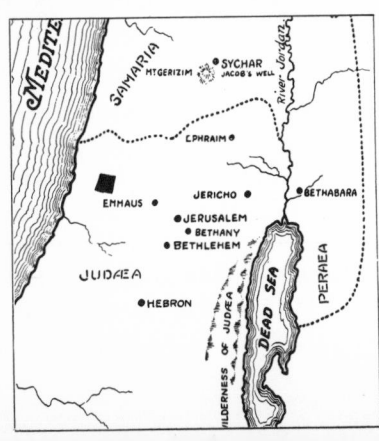

98— RAMLEH (ARIMATHAEA)

About four miles west of Lydda, and some 10 miles from Joppa, in the midst of Sharon, is the beautiful little city of Ramleh, which was called Arimathaea in Jesus' day. Jesus was buried in the new tomb of Joseph of Arimathaea, in which no one had been buried previously. This Joseph lived here and the splendid little church over there is dedicated to his memory. (Matt. 27:57.)

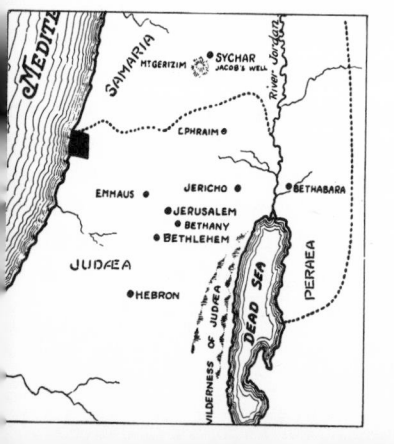

99— JOPPA

And this brings us to the end of our journey west—Joppa. Here we find ourselves immediately surrounded by places made sacred by the occurrence of Bible events: (1) Rafts of Cedars of Lebanon, for Solomon's Temple, were landed at Joppa. (2 Chron. 2.) (2) Jonah shipped from here when he tried to run away from the Lord (Jonah 1), and (3) Dorcas was restored to life by Peter here. (Acts 9:36.) (See map.)

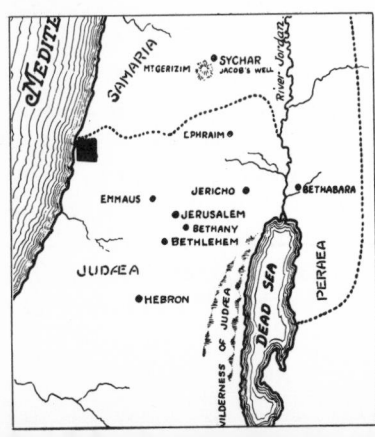

100— HOUSE OF SIMON THE TANNER

When Peter went to Joppa to restore Dorcas to life, he abode with one Simon, a tanner, who lived in a house overlooking the sea. Here is a house by the sea-shore, an old tanning vat, and a well beside it, and the steps leading to the roof. So this is pointed out as the very "House of Simon" with whom Peter lodged while in Joppa at this time. (Acts 10.)

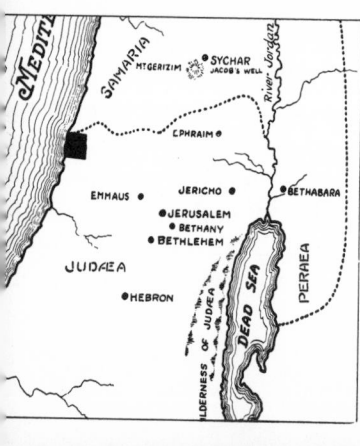

101— THE HOUSE TOP

This is the top of the house we have just seen and is reached by the steps we saw from the court. Peter was favored by the tanner, who permitted him to sleep here. One day while Peter was on this roof, he saw a wonderful vision, which sent him to Caesarea, where he made the first Gentile converts, Cornelius and his house. (Acts 10.) The beautiful Mediterranean spreads itself out before us.

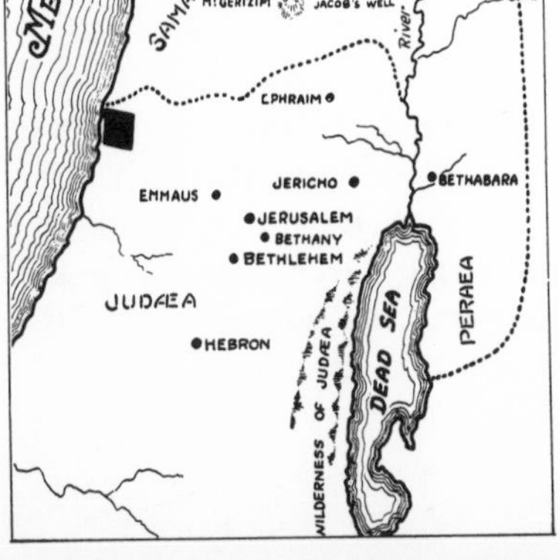

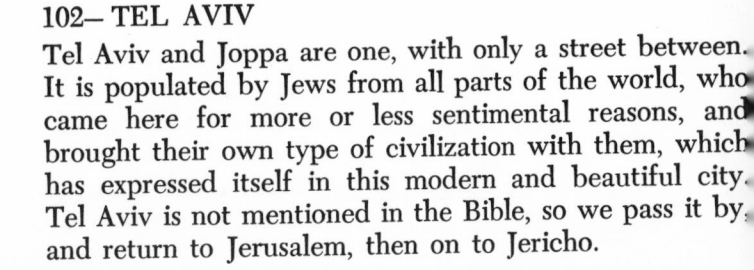

102— TEL AVIV

Tel Aviv and Joppa are one, with only a street between.
It is populated by Jews from all parts of the world, who
came here for more or less sentimental reasons, and
brought their own type of civilization with them, which
has expressed itself in this modern and beautiful city.
Tel Aviv is not mentioned in the Bible, so we pass it by,
and return to Jerusalem, then on to Jericho.

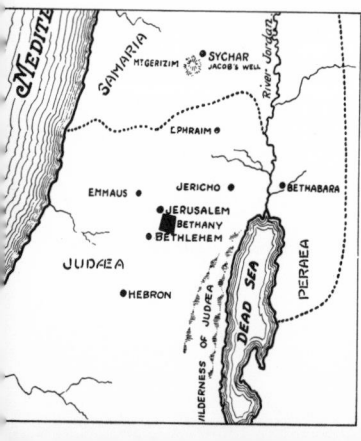

103– OLIVET – EAST SIDE

Now we will move on to Jericho. Directly over the hill, and exactly opposite the place we stand, is the Holy City. So here we see the Tower on Olivet from the east side. Jesus was on that hill several times and finally ascended into Heaven from its summit. Notice the husband rides, while the wife walks, carrying the burden. That is the way they do it over there.

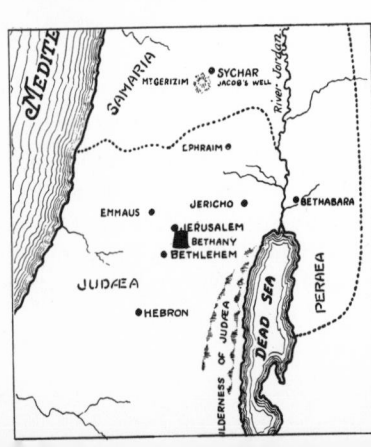

104— BETHANY

Here in Bethany, Jesus visited Martha and Mary, and
raised Lazarus from the dead. Jesus also healed Simon
a leper, here, and the ruins of the leper's house are on
the hill. Martha served a dinner for Jesus in Simon'
house and her sister, Mary, anointed him with preciou
ointment. (John 11.) (See the map.)

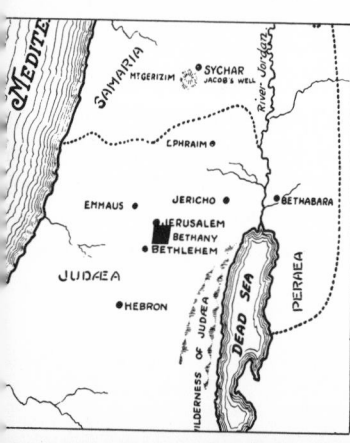

105— CHURCH OF THE LORD'S PRAYER

While Jesus was in Bethany on one of his visits, he went out on Olivet alone, to pray, and his Disciples came to him and asked him to teach them to pray also. Then he began: "Our Father which art in Heaven . . ." So it was here that Jesus, himself, uttered "The Lord's Prayer" as we have it today, for the first time, and this church stands on the spot where it occurred. (Luke 11:1.)

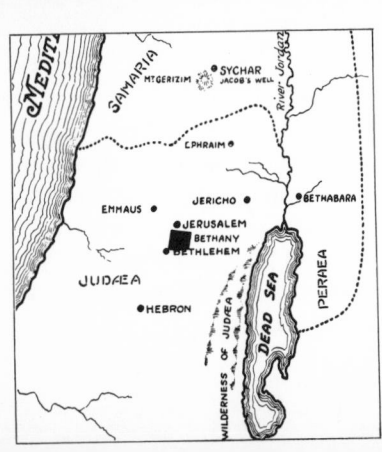

106— BETHPHAGE

This picture was made from the Tower on Olivet. The church in the foreground is Bethphage, where the colt upon which Jesus rode on his "Triumphal Entry" was secured. (Matt. 21:1.) Bethany lies just beyond, and the Wilderness of Judaea stretches out before us to the Dead Sea, which lies silently at the foot of the purple mountains of Moab, in the distance.

107—ON THE JERICHO ROAD

The Jericho Road, winding its way through the desert hills before us, was the highway pursued by the man who "fell among thieves," and was picked up and cared for by "The Good Samaritan." The "Wise Men from the East," on their search for the Baby Jesus, must have also traveled this very same road, and Herod the Great, who rebuilt Jericho, has passed over it many times.

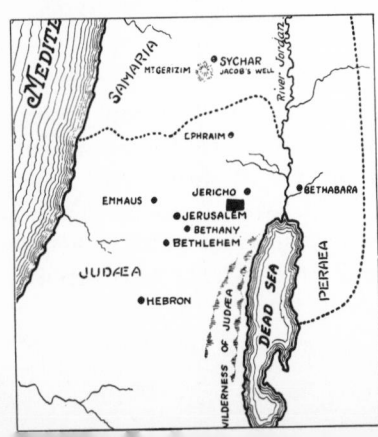

108— THE GOOD SAMARITAN'S INN

And here is the inn, the old caravansary, the half-way house between Jerusalem and Jericho. The man who fell among thieves was treated by a Samaritan, and cared for at the inn, until he recovered. This is the inn, and it is likely identical with the one in which Jesus was born in Bethlehem, except for the new part which faces the road. (Luke 10:25.)

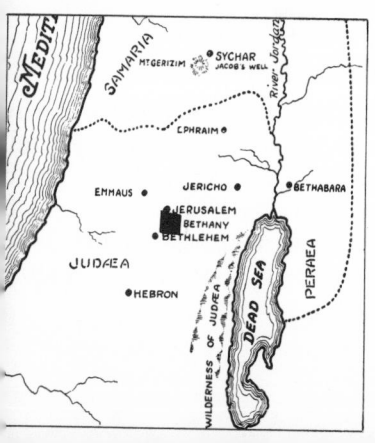

109— BROOK CHERITH

This great chasm, called "The Brook Cherith," flows across the Valley of Jericho to the River Jordan. When Jezebel, the wicked Queen of Ahab, swore vengeance against Elijah in Samaria, he fled here to this brook. He was fed by ravens and drank from the brook, until it dried up, and then he fled to Zarephath, far to the north of Mt. Carmel. (I Kings 17:3.)

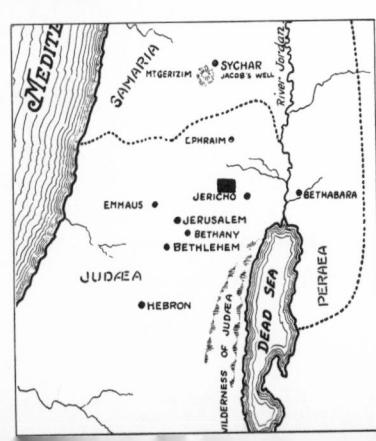

110— ELIJAH'S MONASTERY (ST. GEORGE)

Far up among the perpendicular and flinty cliffs of the Brook Cherith, you see this great Monastery of St. George, clinging to the rocks, built as a memorial to the great Prophet, Elijah, who was fed by ravens here and escaped starvation. (I Kings 17.) On the summit of the hill, Jesus fasted 40 days and was tempted by Satan immediately following his baptism. (Mark 1.)

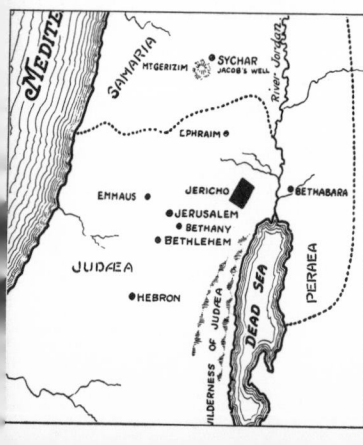

111— JORDAN VALLEY

From a slight elevation above Elijah's Monastery, we get a beautiful view of the naturally fertile valley of Jordan. Sodom once stood over there. Lot lived there and was taken prisoner. (Gen. 13.) Sodom was destroyed by fire and brimstone, and Lot's wife was turned to a pillar of salt, on that plain. The Jordan is in sight.

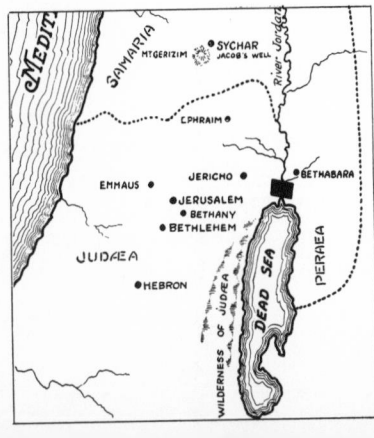

112— RIVER JORDAN

And here it is, the River Jordan. When Moses died near here, and Joshua took charge and led the people across the Jordan at this point, the water separated and "They crossed on dry land." (Joshua 3:14.) Elijah and Elisha crossed here in the same fashion. John the Baptist preached to the people and this is pointed out as the exact spot where our Lord was baptized. (Mark 1.)

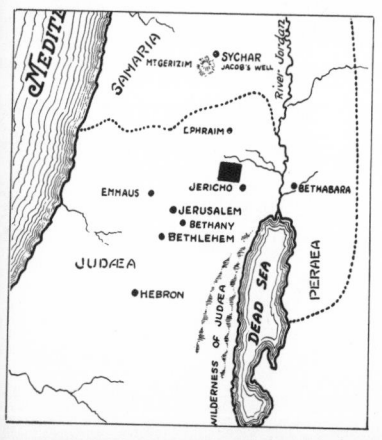

113— QUARANTINIA (MT. OF TEMPTATION)

This mountain, Quarantinia, is 5 or 6 miles west from where we just stood on the banks of Jordan. Jesus was led by the Spirit to this hill-top where he fasted 40 days, and was tempted by Satan, immediately following his baptism. (Luke 4:1.) We also left Elijah up there a few minutes ago, where he was in hiding from the wicked Jezebel of Israel. (I Kings 17.) The water is from Elisha's Spring. (2 Kings 2.)

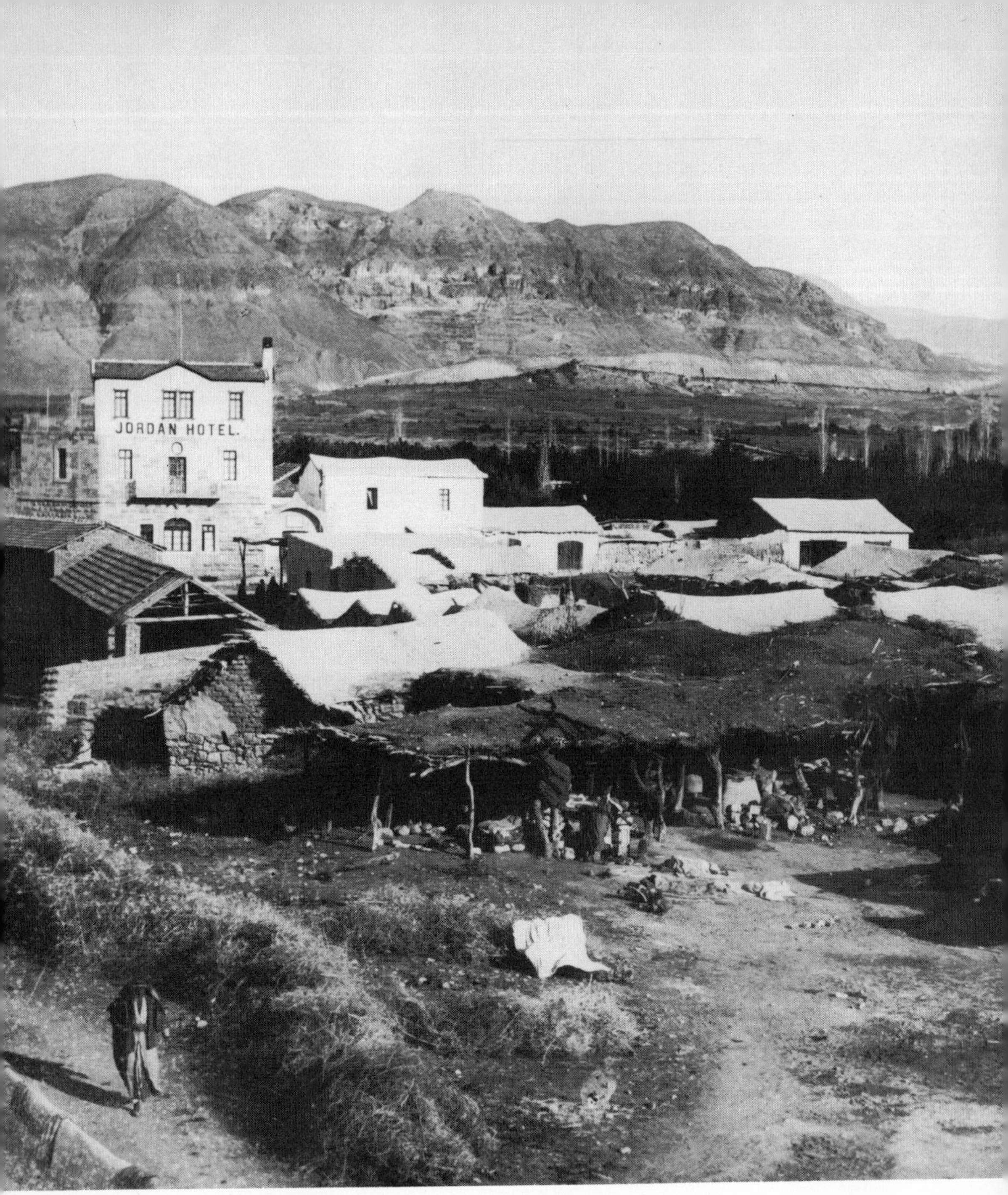

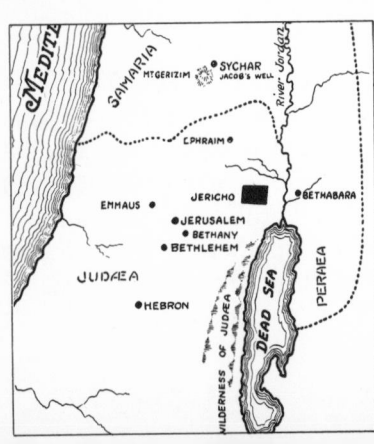

114— MODERN JERICHO

The mountain is Quarantinia, the village is modern Jericho, and the Jordan is back of us. As Jesus came into this place on his last trip to Jerusalem, he called Zachaeus, out of a tree, and abode with him over night. Jesus healed blind Bartimaeus here. (Luke 19:1.) King Herod died here of a loathsome and incurable disease.

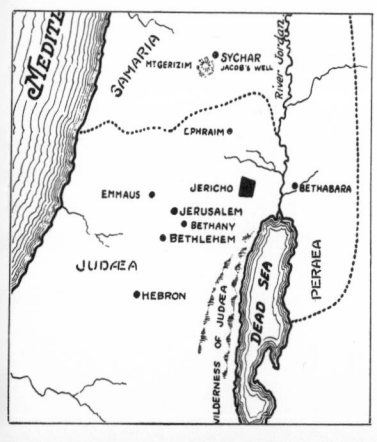

115— RUINS OF JERICHO

The Jericho of Jushua's day was here at the foot of Quarantinia, three miles from the modern city. When Joshua marched around Jericho the required number of times, "The walls fell flat," and here it is. He destroyed every living thing, except the family of Rahab. Achan stole a slug of gold from the plunder and was stoned to death in the Valley of Achor. (Joshua 6.)

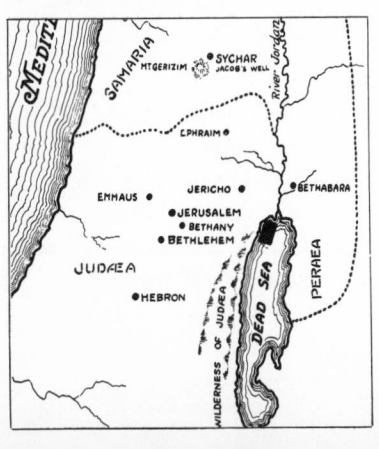

116— THE DEAD SEA

The Dead Sea lies in the deepest hole in the earth's surface—1300 feet. Sea level is 80 miles north at Lake Hulah. If the water from the Red Sea should break over, there would be no Dead Sea, River Jordan, or Sea of Galilee. From brim to bottom, there are beds of salt, and great hills of it on the shores—that is why the man floats.

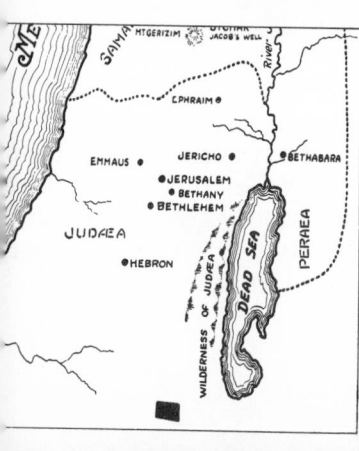

117— MOUNT SIER

After Jacob had filched Esau's birthright, he tried to escape his brother's wrath by leaving the country. He went to his uncle, Laban, at Haran. Esau also tried to lose himself here in Mt. Sier, which is called Edom, "Red" (Esau). But in spite of its barrenness, he prospered, and by the time Jacob returned, he was a rich man.

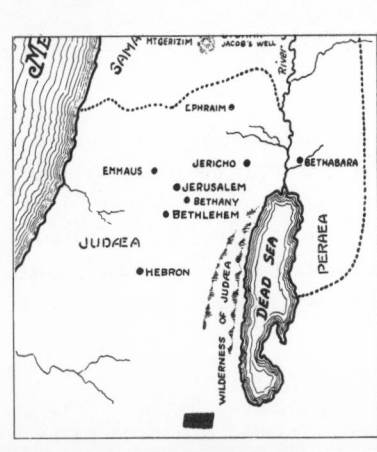

118— LAHAI-ROI

This spring is pointed out as the exact spot where Esau sold his birthright to Jacob for a mess of pottage. (Gen. 27.) The twins were born here. (Gen. 24.) Hagar and Ishmael almost famished from thirst, when they discovered this very spring in Mt. Sier. Ishmael grew up among these hills and has been "a thorn in the flesh" of Israel to this day. (Gen. 21.)

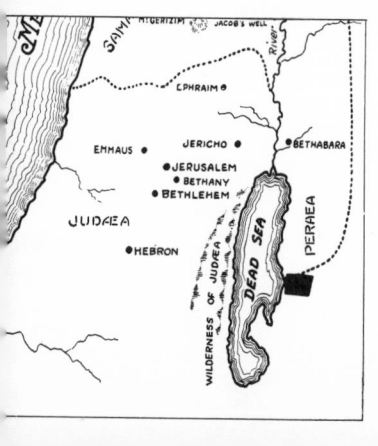

119— THE ARNON RIVER

The boundary between Moab and the Ammorites is the River Arnon, and here is the mouth of it. So when Israel crossed this little streamlet, they immediately found themselves in trouble. (Num. 21:13.) They were attacked by Sihon, the king, who was overwhelmingly defeated at Jahaz and driven back to the waters of Heshbon, by Israel. (Num. 21.)

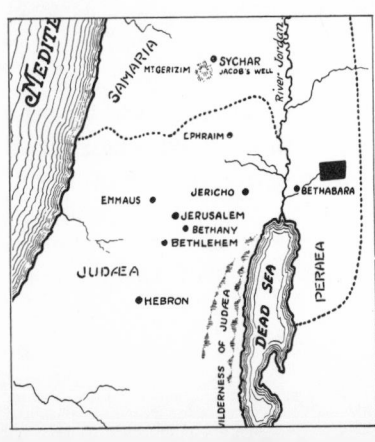

120— AMMAN

Originally this country east of Jordan was called Ammon, named for the second son of Lot, by his own daughter. In Jesus' day it was called Peraea and today it is known as Jordan. The present capital is Amman, pictured here. The name of this town in Jesus' time was Philadelphia, which is referred to as one of the Seven Churches mentioned in Revelation 1:11.

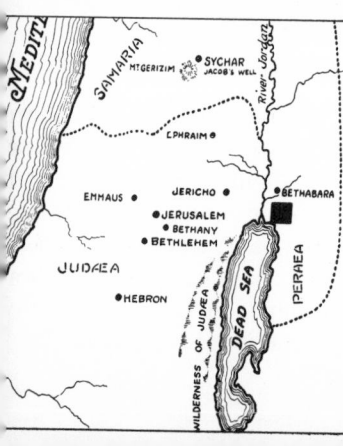

121— MACHAERUS

An early tradition claims that the city of Machaerus once stood here, and there are the ruins of the prison in which John the Baptist was incarcerated by Herod Antipas. It is not far from Mt. Nebo, near the Dead Sea, where we go next.

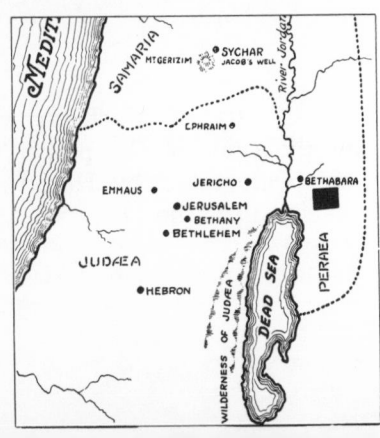

122— MOUNT NEBO

Mt. Nebo is the highest point in Trans-Jordania. It looks down upon the Dead Sea and across it into Canaan, or Palestine, then referred to as "The Promised Land." Moses stood here and viewed "the land of milk and honey," which he was not permitted to enter, and as the sun was going down, his physical sun set, and he was buried here by the hand of the Lord. (Deut. 34:1.) Elijah likely came here also when he was carried to Heaven in a chariot of fire. (2 Kings 2:11.)

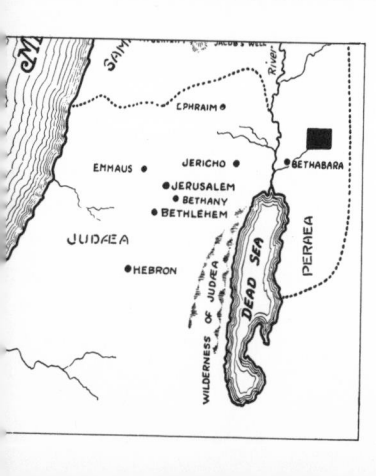

123— SCENE IN PERAEA

This entire country was destroyed and its population annihilated by Joshua, and East Jordan was allotted to Reuben, Gad and Manasseh. But when Jesus was here, it was called Peraea. Here he told the stories of "The Prodigal Son," "The Good Samaritan," "The Rich Young Ruler," "The Rich Man and Lazarus," and many others. (The map.)

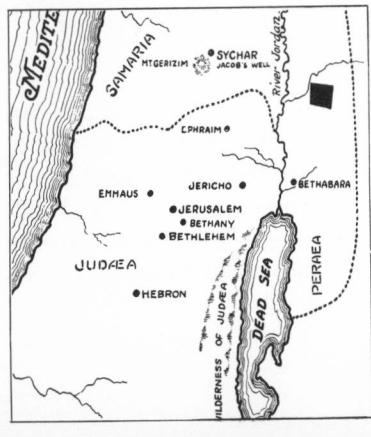

124— RAMOTH-GILEAD

Ramoth-Gilead is one of the largest cities of the East
Jordan country. It is probably the native city of Elijah and
where he was living when he heard of the idolatry of
Ahab and Jezebel. The running battle in which Ahab was
mortally wounded started from here. (2 Kings 8:28.)

125— THE JABBOK RIVER

When Jacob arrived at this point on the Jabbok, in his flight from Laban, his father-in-law, he sent his family to the other side, and prayed all night. His name was changed to Israel (Prevailed), right here, and the next day he met Esau, who, in spite of the past, received him as a real brother, and offered his services in any capacity that Jacob might request. (Gen. 32.)

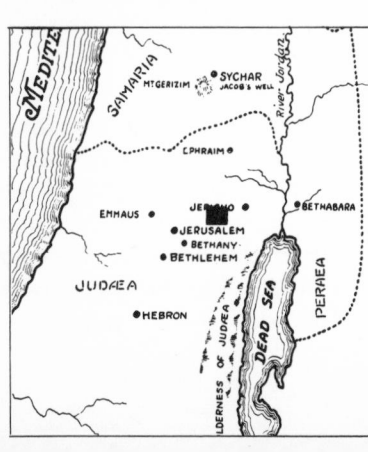

126— AIN-FARAH

This is one of the few perennial streams in Palestir
Shepherds, including David, once brought their floc
here in summer, because it is the only water of any sizab
quantity. From scenes of his shepherd life here, Dav
based his Twenty-third Psalm. And to the visitor to th
beautiful streamlet, it seems reasonable to say that t
entire Psalm is illustrated by scenes along the brook.

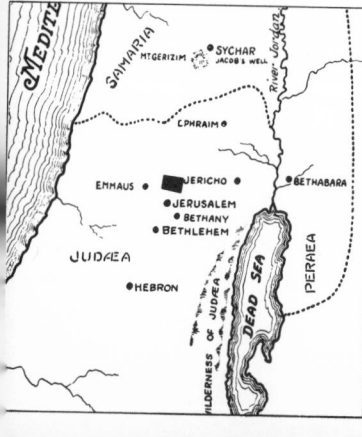

127— ANATHOTH

Anathoth is 3 or 4 miles from Jerusalem and from here we begin our journey northward. It is the birthplace of both Jeremiah (Jer. 1), and Abiather, the High Priest in David's day. Abiather joined Joab in an effort to elevate Adonijah to the throne of David. So when Solomon became king, a few days later, he had both Joab and Adonijah put to death, and Abiather was exiled here at Anathoth. (I Kings 2.)

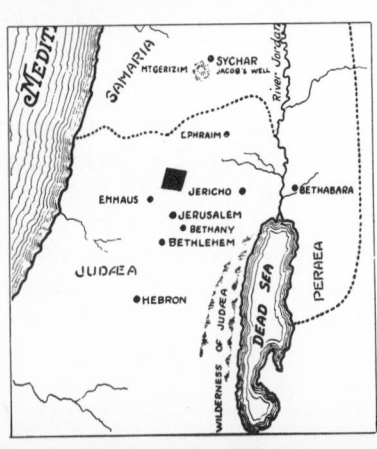

128— GIBEAH OF SAUL

Gibeah lies in the background. It was the first capital of Saul after he became king; here David played his harp to soothe him, Jonathan became David's friend, and Michael, Saul's daughter, became his wife. Nob, city of the priests, was a suburb where 79 of them were be-headed by Saul because they favored David when he fled from Saul. (I Sam. 21.)

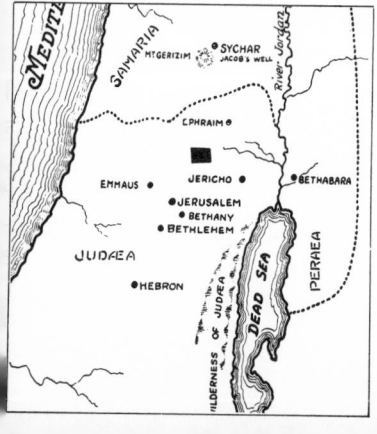

129— MIZPAH

The principal places in the Holy Land today are connected by roads like this, and as compared with those of a few years ago, we might say they are "perfect." But there is more to this picture than the mere road. Mizpah, one of the most important cities in Israel, in that day, was located on that highest, distant hill. It was also the home of the great Prophet, Samuel.

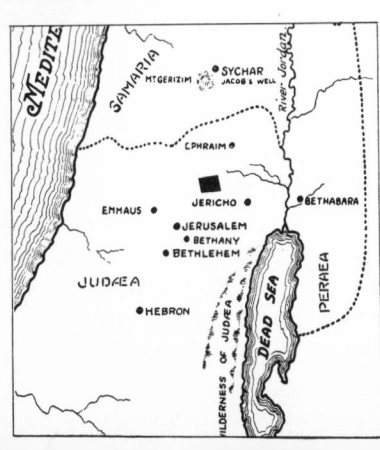

130— MIZPAH

The building on the hill covers "The Tomb of Samuel."
It replaces an old mosque, which was destroyed in the
First World War and is much more imposing than the
first. Samuel was a Prophet and judged Israel here for
many years. It was while he lived in Mizpah that he
anointed Saul first King of Israel, somewhere within the
neighborhood of this hillside before you. (I Sam. 10.)

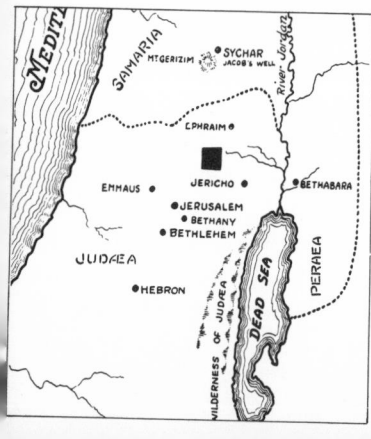

131— BETHEL

This is Bethel, 12 miles north of Jerusalem. When Abraham came over from Padan-Aram, he encountered a drouth here, and continued on to Egypt, where he denied his wife. Here Jacob saw "the ladder let down from Heaven, and angels ascending and descending." (Gen. 28.) Jeroboam set up two golden calves in Israel; one at Dan, and the other here at Bethel. (I Kings 12.)

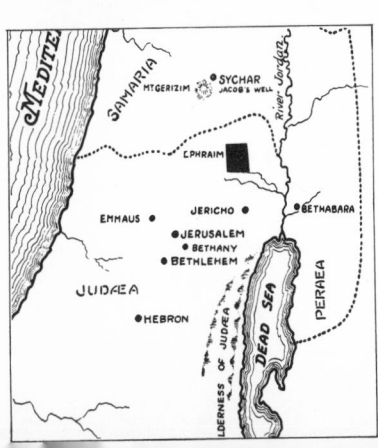

132— EPHRAIM

Deborah lived here in Ephraim when she called Barak from Kadesh to meet her on Mt. Tabor, to plan a campaign against Sisera. The battle took place at the River Kishon and only Sisera escaped, but in a few days he was murdered by another woman at Megiddo. (Judges 4.) Jesus also came here for a few days, after he raised Lazarus from the dead in Bethany. (John 11.)

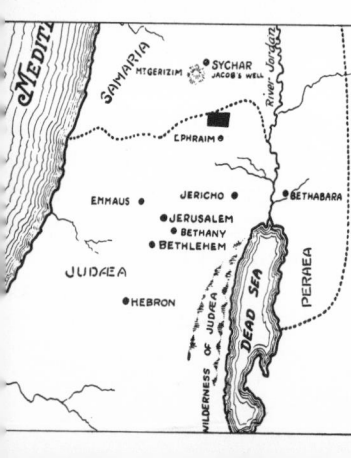

133— BAAL-HAZOR

Absalom invited his half-brother, Amnon, to a sheep-shearing feast at Hazor, and in the midst of a drunken carousel, prearranged by Absalom, Amnon was slain, and Absalom fled to his grandfather at Gesher. (2 Sam. 13.) Absalom's sister, Tamar, had been wronged by Amnon, who left her in disgrace, and this gave rise to the terrible incident between the two sons of David.

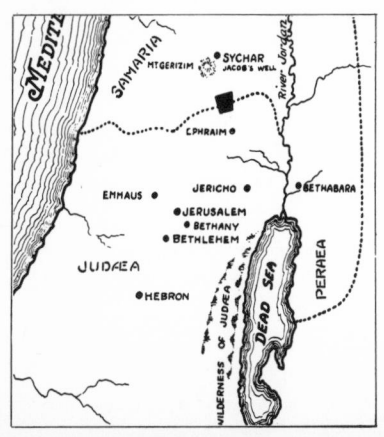

134— SHILOH

After Joshua had conquered the Canaanites, he brough
the Tabernacle from Gilgal here to Shiloh, which becam
the center of worship in Israel, and continued for 3C
years. The last Priest to officiate here was Eli. When th
Ark of the Covenant was taken into battle against th
Philistines, and captured, Eli fell from his chair an
broke his neck. (Joshua 18:1.) Hannah dedicated her so
Samuel, to the Lord here, and he was brought up by E

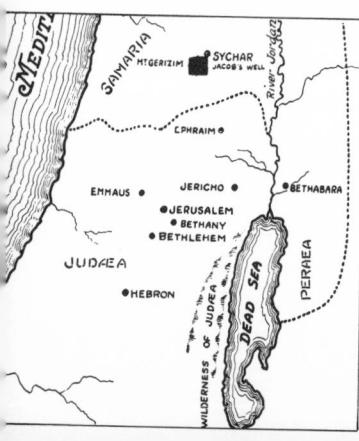

135— PLAIN OF MOREH (SHECHEM)

The first stopping place of Abraham in Palestine was on this Plain of Moreh (Shechem), where he built the first altar for Hebrew worship. (Gen. 12.) Jacob lived here several years and dug a well, which is located at the foot of the hill (right), and here he also buried the idols stolen from Laban, in Padan-Aram. (Gen. 35.) (Black square on map.)

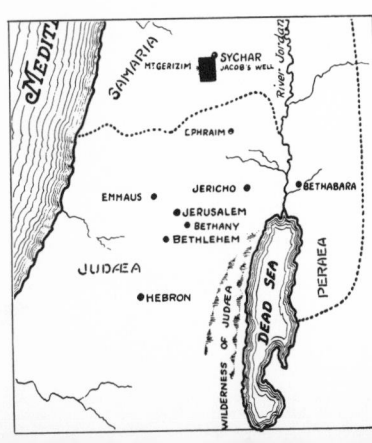

136— JACOB'S WELL

When Jesus was here, he met a Woman of Sychar, and
asked her for a drink of water, which he apparently did
not get. (John 4:5.) The woman said: "The well is very
deep," and its depth is estimated at about 100 feet. The
people invited Jesus to Sychar and he accepted their
invitation and taught them for two days, with splendid
results. This is a woman of Sychar.

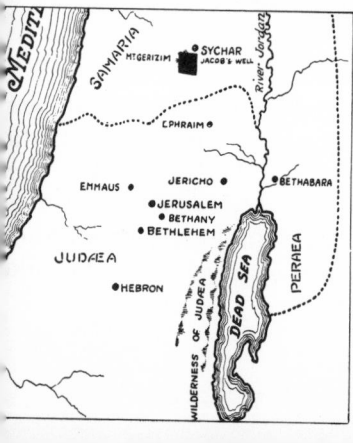

137— SYCHAR

We are now in the village of Sychar and the well is over against the foot of the hill, called Mt. Gerizim. When Jesus discussed with the woman "The Water of Life," she did not understand it and when she spoke about Jews worshipping in Jerusalem, but the Samaritans, "in this mountain," she referred to the Temple over there (the mere dot), up on the summit of Gerizim. (John 4.)

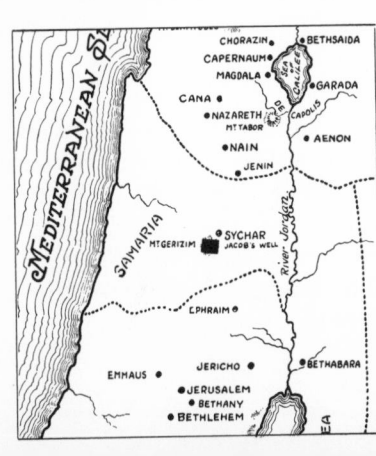

138— SAMARITAN TEMPLE

And this is the Temple just mentioned. The Samaritans meet here on Mt. Gerizim once a year, and the group you see consists of about all the able-bodied men who have the strength to attend. Most of these oldsters are married to little girls, who are mere children, and one day soon there will be no Samaritans. The entire 100 of them live in Shechem.

139— JOSEPH'S TOMB

Four hundred years before Israel escaped from Egypt, they promised Joseph (upon his dying request), that they would bury his mummy in Shechem. And true to their promise, they carried his body through their wanderings in the Wilderness, and when Joshua arrived here, he had Joseph buried, as his forefathers had promised. Joseph's body, supposedly, lies under the dome.

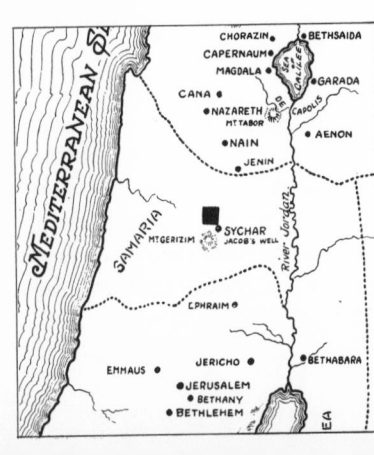

140— SHECHEM

Gradually, from time to time, Shechem has crept up this valley until now it is some 2 or 3 miles above Moreh where it stood in the days of Jacob and Abraham. Gideon lived near here and refused to be king, but his son Abimelech, did try it, and failed. The people ran him out of town, but before he left he sowed the valley with salt, and fled to Tirzah.

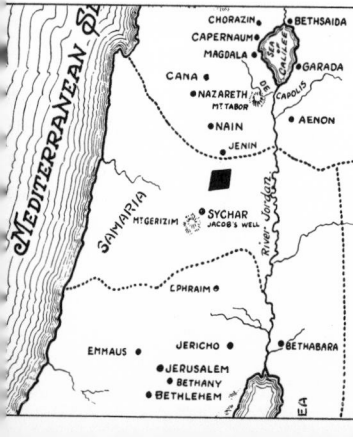

141— TIRZAH

At Tirzah, Abimelech was fatally wounded by a woman, and he demanded his bodyguard to slay him rather than die at the hand of a woman. The story of Tirzah's kings that followed was one of intrigue and murder. Abijah, Baasha, and Elah passed in rapid succession, and when the army crowned Omri, Zimri burned the city and perished in its flames. (I Kings 16.)

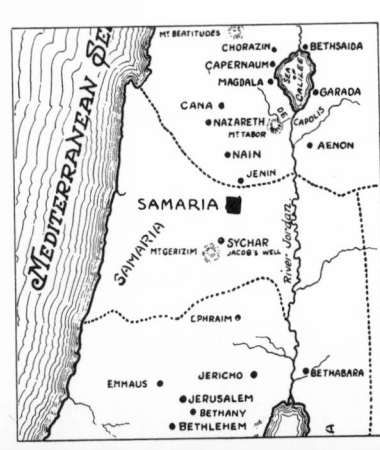

142— SAMARIA

Samaria stands on the hill, but when Omri arrived, there
was no population. He built the city of Samaria, which
out-rivaled all its neighbors. Since that day, volumes of
historical events have occurred in this city. It has been
destroyed and rebuilt, again and again, and each time it
became more beautiful than before; until now.

143— OMRI'S PALACE (RUINS)

Omri lived in an Ivory Palace. He was the father of Ahab, and he selected a wife for him from the family of Ethbaal, King of Sidon. She was Jezebel, the most despicable character mentioned in the Bible. She encountered Elijah and cursed him to his face. She made promises only to break them, and murdered just to see the blood flow. (1 Kings 18.)

144— A STREET IN SAMARIA

In the days of the Prophets, Amos and Hosea cursed the city, and it did not recover until the days of Herod the Great. Herod rebuilt and beautified Samaria, as these columns indicate. Many of the streets were covered with artistic roofs, supported by shafts of marble, like these. But after Herod's horrible death, nobody cared, so this is what you see today.

145— CHURCH OF JOHN THE BAPTIST

John the Baptist had been a prisoner in Macheraes, near Mt. Nebo, for a long time, when Herod Antipas had him beheaded. His body was buried at Macheraes and his head was buried in Samaria, and this Church was erected over its burial place. Philip preached here in Samaria after the first persecution in Jerusalem, and Simon Magus was denounced by Peter. (Acts 9.)

146— DOTHAN

Dothan is about 12 miles north of Samaria. Here Joseph visited his brothers, who dropped him into a well to die but finally he was lifted out and sold into slavery. (Gen 37:17.) The Prophet, Elisha, prayed for his servant's spiritual eyes to be opened and he saw a vision—a heavenly host, on that mountain-top—coming to their rescue. (Kings 6:17.)

147— CAESAREA

Caesarea, over on the Mediterranean coast, was the home of Cornelius, a Roman Centurion, who became the first Gentile convert to the Christian faith, through the preaching of Peter. (Acts 10.) Paul was also brought to Caesarea from Jerusalem when his life was threatened by the Jews. And, for apparently no reason at all, he was cast into prison, where he remained two years, while he waited for his appeal to Rome. (Acts, chapters 23-26.)

148— BETHSHAN AND GILBOA

The mountain is Gilboa, where all the sons of Saul, except one, were killed, his army totally defeated, and the King himself committed suicide. (1 Sam. 28:4.) The Philistines' camp was here at Bethshan, and when they found the bodies of the King and his sons, they beheaded them all and nailed their naked bodies to the walls of Bethshan. (1 Sam. 31.)

149— GIDEON'S FOUNTAIN

When Gideon called for volunteers to drive out maurad-
ers, who carried their crops away, 30,000 men volunteered.
But Gideon, who preferred to give the victory to the
power of God, put a test to the 30,000 here at this Spring,
and when only 300 qualified, he armed them with "torches
and pitchers." When the pitchers were broken, the torches
so confused the enemy that they fled in disorder. Read
Judges 7.

150— TOWER OF JEZREEL

Ahab and Jezebel spent some of their time here at Jezreel. When Elijah, at Ramoth-Gilead, heard of their spiritual depravity, he came here and denounced them to their faces. The King and Queen also waited here while Elijah called fire down upon his sacrifice at Mt. Carmel. (1 Kings 18.) After the murder of Ahab, Jezebel was thrown from the upper window of the Tower of Jezreel, and she was consumed by dogs. (2 Kings 9.)

151— JENIN

After Jesus raised Lazarus from the dead in Bethany, he tarried a short time at Ephraim. Then as he was making his way to Peraea, he passed through this beautiful village of Jenin (tradition), and healed the Ten Lepers. Originally Jenin may have been ancient Gur, where Jehu slew Ahazia, the King, (Jezebel's son), and took over. (See map.)

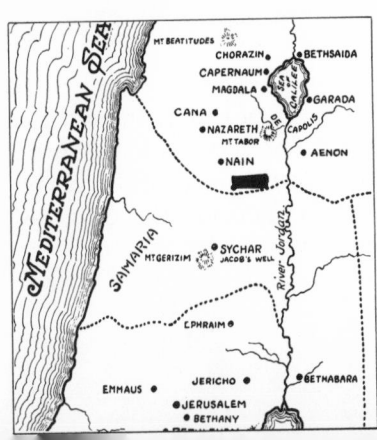

152— SHUNEM

Next we will see Shunem, which lies just across the Plain of Esdraelon, from Jenin. Elisha often visited here and the good family who had received spiritual favors from him, furnished a room and he was always welcome. Later he raised their son from a sunstroke. (2 Kings 4.) Shunem was also the home of a fair maiden, Abishag, who was selected to minister to David in his last days. (1 Kings 1.)

153— ENDOR

Endor is also located at the foot of Mt. Moreh, where the bewildered King Saul engaged a witch to call Elijah from the dead, to advise him. So she called Elijah, who informed Saul of the evil day that was soon to come and his prediction was correct. (1 Sam. 28.)

154— MOUNT MOREH AND ESDRAELON

The Plain is Esdraelon. The hill in the distance is Moreh. Esdraelon is the most fertile plain and the most blood-drenched spot in Palestine. To the right flows the River Jordan. To the left is the Mediterranean, and the Kishon separates them from Mount Carmel.

155— MOUNT CARMEL AND THE SEA

Mt. Carmel forms one of the most striking and characteristic features of Palestine. Here it juts itself out into the Mediterranean at a height of 600 feet. Many activities of Elijah and Elisha occurred on Mt. Carmel; their School of the Prophets was here, and fire fell on Elijah's sacrifice on this mountain. (1 Kings 18.) (Keep up with the maps.)

156— PLACE OF SACRIFICE

Elijah challenged Ahab and Jezebel to the test. The God of Elijah, or Jezebel's god (Baal). The God who answered "with fire" was to be accepted as the true Deity. The hundreds of Prophets of Baal prayed, but no fire fell. When Elijah prayed, "fire fell, and consumed his sacrifice," and the Prophet destroyed the Priests of Baal. (1 Kings 18:40.) The monument stands on the spot where Elijah's altar stood.

157— THE RIVER KISHON

This little streamlet flows by the base of Mt. Carmel and when Elijah slew the hundreds of Priests of Baal, on the mountain side, the River ran red with their blood. Barak and Deborah also met Sisera's army in this valley and destroyed every man in it except Sisera himself. This, of course, was hundreds of years before Elijah destroyed the Prophets of Baal here. (Judges 4.)

158— MEGIDDO (ARMAGEDDON)

When Sisera escaped the sword of Barak, he fled here to Megiddo and sought refuge in the tent of Jael. She gave him a hearty reception. But while he slept in her tent, she drove a tent pin through his temples, so the very last member of the Army of Jabin died. (Judges 4.) Centuries later, Joash, King of Jerusalem, was slain here by Egypt's Necho. (2 Kings 23:29.)

159— CARMELITE MONASTERY

As we have previously noticed, Mt. Carmel rises up out of the Plain of Esdraelon and juts out into the sea over Haifa; and this Monastery stands near the end looking over on to the sea and Haifa. Although Mt. Carmel is held sacred by Mohammedan, Jew, and Christian alike, the Carmelite Monks operate it, and it is dedicated to the great Prophets, Elijah and Elisha.

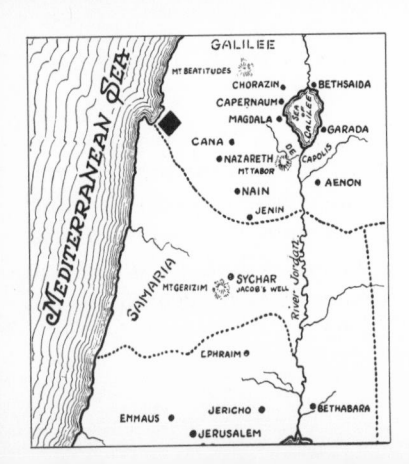

160— HAIFA

From the Monastery, we will step out on the brink of the hill, and here at our feet, is Haifa, an ultra-modern city of Israel. It has a good harbor, some great oil pipelines from the east pour millions of barrels of oil into its tanks, and everything is as modern as you will find in any American city. The Bay is called Akka, and on the other shore is Ptolemais.

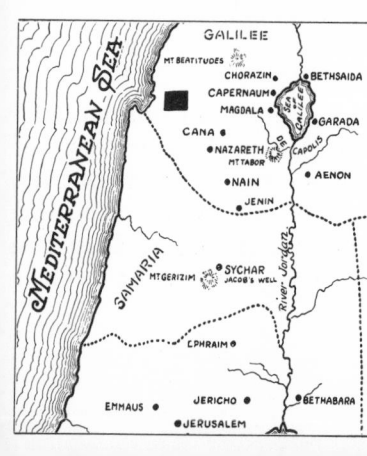

161— PTOLEMAIS

Toward the end of Paul's last voyage to Jerusalem, his ship anchored here at Ptolemais, and he went ashore and saluted the Church. In the words of Acts 21:7, "And when we had finished our course from Tyre, we came to Ptolemais and saluted the brethren, and abode with them one day. And the next day we departed, and came unto Caesarea."

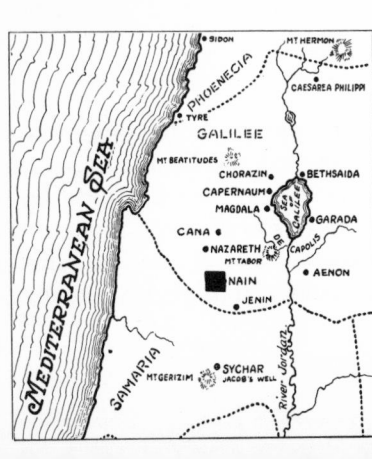

162— NAIN

Soon after Jesus delivered "The Sermon On The Mount," he went to the village of Nain, about 15 miles south of Capernaum. As they were entering the gates of the city, they met a funeral procession. The only son of a widow was being buried, but Jesus restored him to life. The people were amazed, "And his Disciples believed." (Luke 7.) The hill is Mt. Tabor.

163— MT. TABOR
Some believe that Mt. Tabor is the place where Jesus was Transfigured, and the beautiful Church, dedicated to this incident, is on its summit. During the days of the Judges, Deborah of Mt. Ephraim, sent for Barak to meet her here with his army of 10,000 men from Kadesh, and on this mountain, they planned their campaign against Sisera. (Judges 4.)

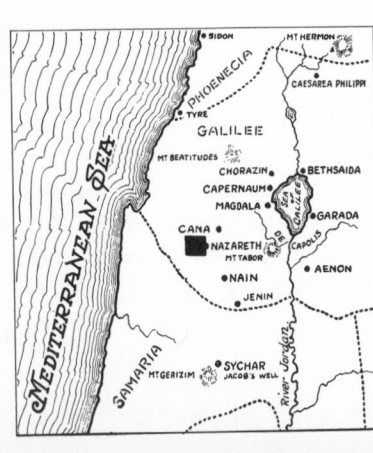

164— NAZARETH HILLS

Here we stand in the road that stretches across the Plain and we are looking up the hill to Nazareth. This is a new Zionist community, in whose hands also is Nazareth. Now we will move up the hill and get a closer view of the city we have heard about since our childhood—Nazareth. (Note the map.)

165— NAZARETH

The most important place in the Holy Land is Nazareth, if we could say one place is more important than another. It is important because Jesus once lived there. Joseph and Mary, though members of the House of Judah, raised their family in this very city. We have all thought, waited, and longed to see this sacred place, and here it is! (Luke 1.)

166— CHURCH OF ANNUNCIATION

"The Church of Annunciation" stands on the spot whe[re] the home of Mary's parents stood. Here, then, the Ang[el] announced to her the coming of the Messiah. (Luke [1]) which makes it one of the most historic places in t[he] world, to every Christian. So the first thing most peo[ple] want to see in Nazareth, is this Church, which has be[en] visited by millions.

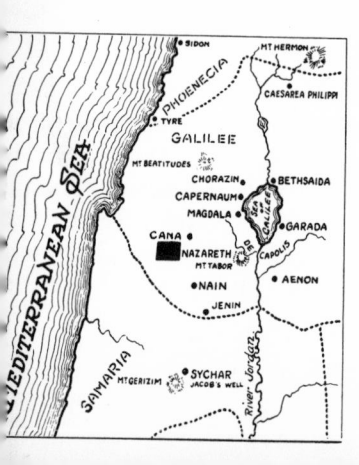

167— THE VIRGIN'S FOUNTAIN

This perennial, gushing Spring is the only source of water supply in the neighborhood. So it is certain that it has been visited by Jesus and his Mother, whose feet have stepped upon this very soil many times. The Palestine traveler will notice that towns are generally built around a natural spring, rather than wells dug after the city has been built, which is true of Nazareth.

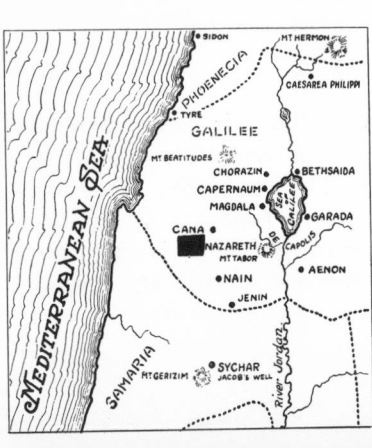

168— HILL PRECIPITATION

Yes, we will always remember Nazareth because of it
living Spring, its Carpenter Shop, its Synagogue, it
Church of Annunciation, and now, this mountain befor
us. Once Jesus was invited to preach in their Synagogue
and because the people disagreed with him, they dru
him away into that mountain-top and tried to cast hi
over the precipice to his death.

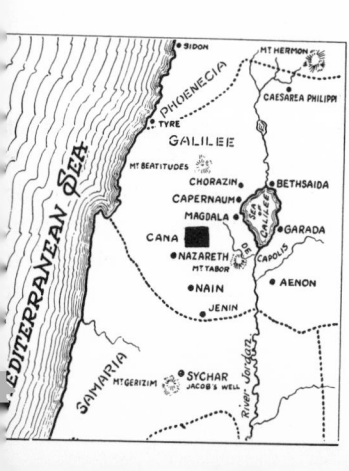

169— CANA OF GALILEE

Cana is just over the hill, about 4 miles from Nazareth. Nathaniel's home was in Cana. Jesus' first miracle (or sign), occurred here when he changed "the water into wine," (John 2), and from here he healed the Nobleman's son who was at the point of death in Capernaum, (John 4.) The Church stands on the spot where the wedding occurred and the water that was changed to wine, was taken from this Spring.

170— SUNRISE ON GALILEE

As we move on eastward over the highest hill, some 170C feet high, we look down upon the Sea of Galilee. As the rising sun casts its golden beams across its blue waters which are here darkened by the shadows of early morning, we observe the real beauty of Blue Galilee. Little wonder Jesus loved it so.

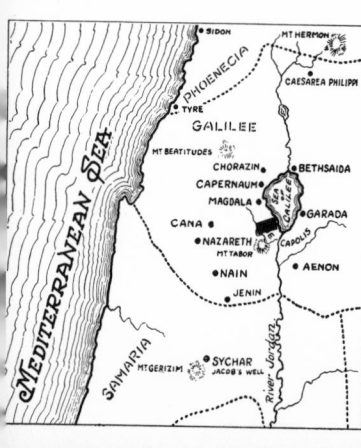

171— TIBERIAS

On the beach stands this beautiful little city of Tiberias. It has no Bible mention because it was in process of construction, by Herod Antipas, in the days of Jesus. This Herod, who was living with his brother's wife, was denounced by John the Baptist here. John was cast into prison, and finally beheaded, to pay the price of Salome's vulgar dance. (Matt. 14.)

172— MAGDALA

After Jesus fed the 4,000 in Decapolis, he came over here to Magdala by boat. But the Pharisees were so contemptuous with him, that he set sail for the other side and did not even remain over night. (Mark 8-10.) Magdala was also the home of Mary Magdalene, who anointed Jesus' feet at Simon's feast in Capernaum, and out of whom Jesus cast seven devils.

173— MT. HATTIN FROM CAPERNAUM

From the beach here at Capernaum, we locate Magdala at the very farthest point to the left, at the foot of the hill. The level part directly in front of us, is the Plain of Gennesaret, and the hill in the distance, is the Mount of Beatitudes. The building among the trees, on the right, is Bethsaida. We will now move over to the Plain of Gennesaret.

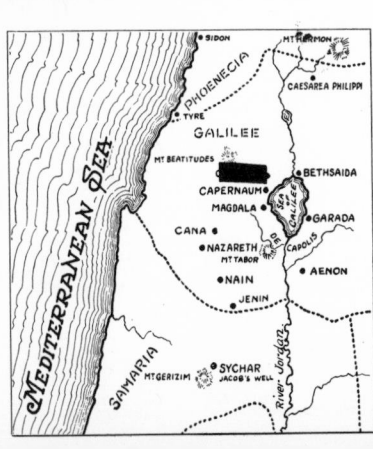

174– PLAIN OF GENNESARET

And here it is. After Jesus fed the 5,000 on the opposit
shore behind us, and walked on the stormy water, h
landed here on Gennesaret and throngs of sick and crip
pled besought him and he healed them all. Jesus als
landed here before he gave "The Sermon On The Mount
and before he ascended the hill, he named "The Twelv
for the first time. (Matt. 4:23.)

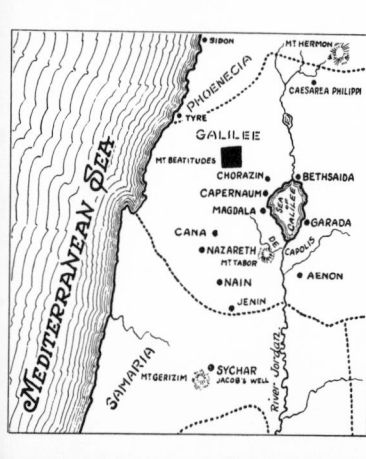

175— MOUNT OF BEATITUDES (HATTIN)
At last we reach the summit of the Mt. of Beatitudes.
"And when he was set, his Disciples came unto him." "The
Sermon On The Mount" followed and it consisted of the
most perfect set of rules for human conduct, ever given
to the world. Jesus (1) delivered blessings, (2) discussed
Christian privileges, and (3) taught them how to pray.
(Matt. 5, 6, 7.)

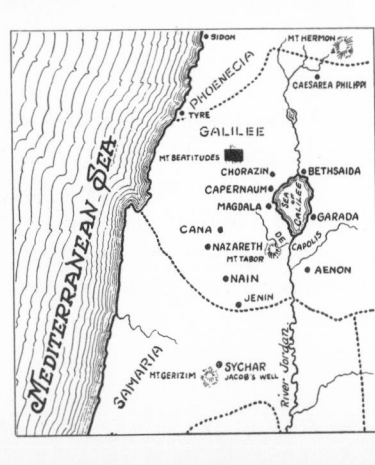

176— MT. HATTIN AND THE SEA

As the multitudes turned to leave the mountain-top, this is what they saw. Down there, 1700 feet below, is the Sea of Galilee, with Capernaum on its north shore. Apparently every one had received a spiritual uplift and were happy. They were prolific in their praises, and exclaimed: "He has taught us as one having authority, and not as the Scribes." (Matt. 7:29.)

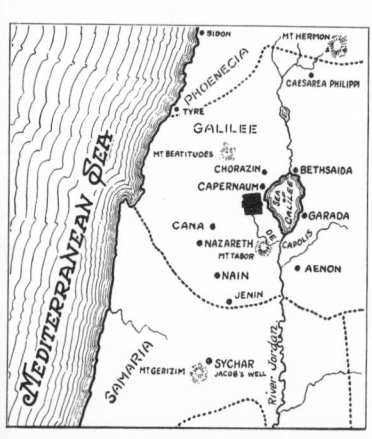

177— BETHSAIDA MONASTERY

As we have noted before, Bethsaida was a suburb of Capernaum, mostly occupied by fishermen. It was the home of James and John, sons of Zebedee. From here we can see almost the entire length of the Sea of Galilee, with Tiberias just beyond the point, and Magdala on this side of the hill. The Mt. of Beatitudes is to the right and Capernaum to the left of us, but out of sight.

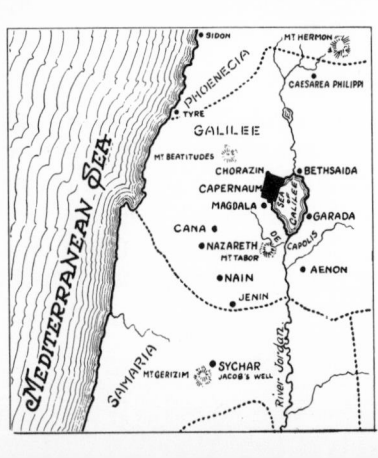

178— BETHSAIDA AND THE BAY

Capernaum lies just beyond the point, and one day when Jesus came around this shore, he called Andrew and Peter to follow him, and when he got a little farther, he called James and John. Now when they cast their net into the waters, right out there before us, as he directed, they caught that miraculous load of fish, that almost sank the boat. (Luke 5:4.)

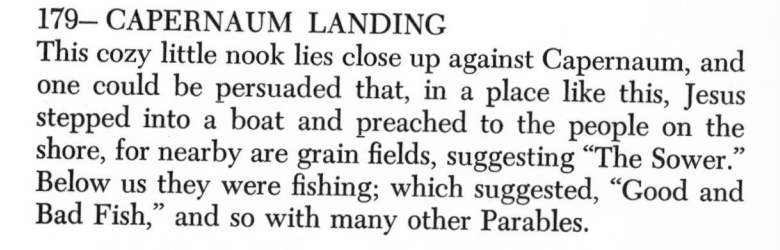

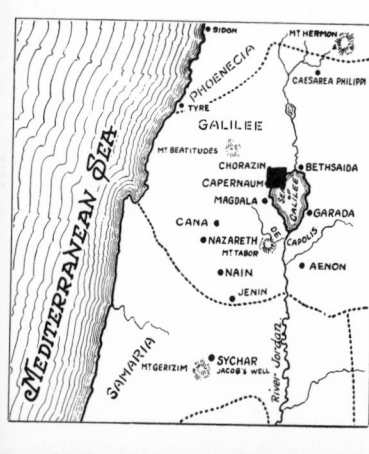

179— CAPERNAUM LANDING

This cozy little nook lies close up against Capernaum, and one could be persuaded that, in a place like this, Jesus stepped into a boat and preached to the people on the shore, for nearby are grain fields, suggesting "The Sower." Below us they were fishing; which suggested, "Good and Bad Fish," and so with many other Parables.

180— THE SYNAGOGUE (RUINS)

One is always thrilled to stand in any spot where Jesus stood, and this is one of those spots. He walked across the floor supported by this foundation, he spoke from its pulpit. He cried: "Come out of him," to the impotent man that sat in his congregation, and "stretch forth your hand," to another, while the Pharisees laid plans to kill him.

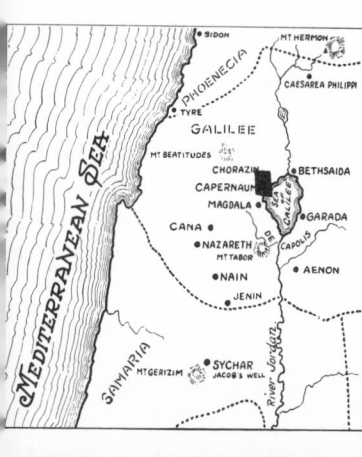

181— STEPS TO THE SYNAGOGUE (RUINS)

The only approach to the meeting room was these steps, which were recently excavated. Acres of what was once called Capernaum were entirely covered by the debris after 20 centuries, and the excavations prove conclusively that when Jesus said, "And thou, Capernaum, which are exalted to heaven, shall be thrust down to hell," (Luke 10:15), that his prophesy was true.

182— SYNAGOGUE RESTORED

The pickaxe has revealed much knowledge of what this beautiful city once was. There are pillars, cornices and capitols, everywhere, making the story complete. This much of the once splendid synagogue has been restored and what you see here has been picked up from the rubbish, piece by piece, and replaced into the same niche it occupied originally.

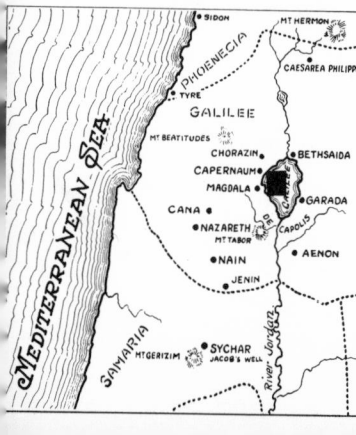

183— TRIP TO GADARA
Everything that we have seen around the Sea of Galilee
has been on the west shore, so now we will go to the east
side. After Jesus had preached his sermon from a boat, he,
and "The Twelve," pushed off in the calm of that evening
for Gadara, over there across the sea, the night he calmed
the storm. (Matt. 8:23-24.)

184— COUNTRY OF THE GADARENES

Next morning they landed here and when they got out into the hills, they met a mad man in a graveyard. He had frightened every person that lived within miles, and he may have attempted to frighten Jesus also. But when Jesus cried: "Come out of the man, thou unclean spirit," he fell at his feet and worshiped him, for he was healed. (Mark 5:8.)

185— MODERN GADARA

The only point east of the Sea of Galilee occupied by modern Israel, is here. It is the same place we saw in the last picture, except the barren hills have been transformed into gardens. Over there you see bee hives, chicken coops, and beef cattle, all together making a general civilized atmosphere. We have not discussed the Jewish situation because that is not our subject.

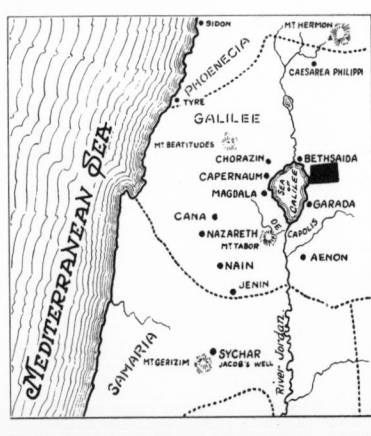

186— BETHSAIDA-JULIUS

This is Bethsaida-Julius. Jesus healed a blind man near this shore (Mark 8:22), and out on that hill, he preached to thousands, and healed the people throughout the entire day. They all became faint with hunger, and he fed 5,000 with a few loaves and fishes. (John 6.) After he healed the blind man here, he went to Caesarea-Philippi. (Black square on map.)

187— SUNRISE ON GALILEE

When the Disciples were crossing the sea, following the feeding of the 5,000, a storm arose and they were frightened. But when Jesus came "walking on the water" here, their fears were gone. And here the sun rises on another day, and we bid farewell to "Blue Galilee, where Jesus loved so much to be." And now we will see next places surrounding Palestine, where many Bible events occurred, which also gives them the right to a place on the list of the Bible Land Family.

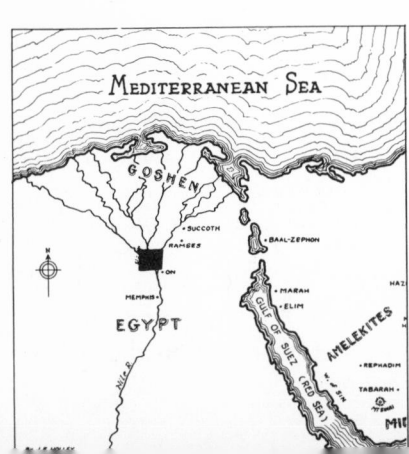

188— THE NILE AND OLD CAIRO

The glorious Nile, life-line of Egypt, flows past old Cairo here. No river in the world is so beautiful, so valuable, or has witnessed so many eventful happenings as the Nile. Its annual overflow makes Egypt a most fertile land, and it has been invaluable as an artery of transportation. Over on that shore, the infant Moses was discovered by Pharaoh's daughter. (Exodus 2.) (Black square on map.)

189— PYRAMIDS OF GIZEH

For many miles before we arrive in Cairo, we catch glimpses of the gigantic Pyramids, but when it is remembered that they stand some 450 feet high, and the base of the large one covers a 14 acre field, we may account for sighting them from such a distance. Each of them cost millions of man hours and a lifetime to build, but no one seems to really know much about them.

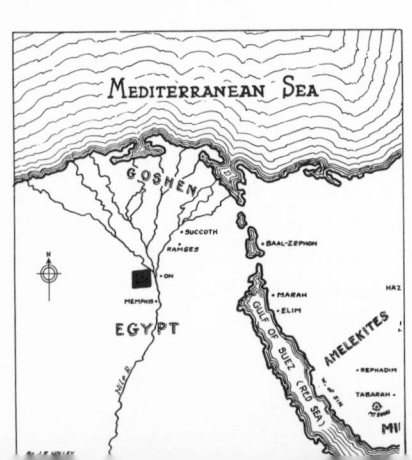

190— THE SPHINX

The reason for this mystifying Sphinx is also wrapped in
as much mystery as its neighbor, the Pyramid. Many
theories have been offered—all different—but they are all
so uncertain that one man's guess is as good as another's
concerning the whys and wherefores of its existence, so
why should we confuse you more by adding another?

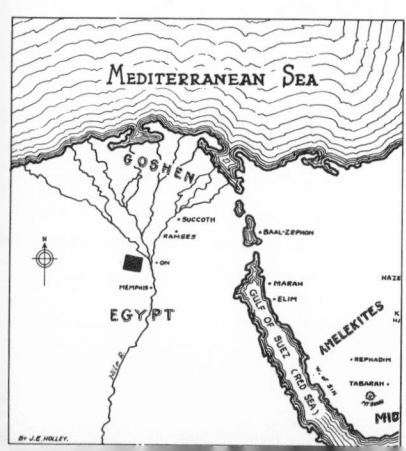

191— THE EXCAVATED SPHINX

The mammoth, crouching lion, with human head, stands some 60 feet in height, and the sprawling body measures 190 feet in length, from tip to toe. There are two apartments in its head, and the interior of the body is reached by a series of steps that lead into a great auditorium which takes up its entire form.

192— FALLEN STATUE OF RAMESES II

Abraham and Sarah traveled these streets when they came here to escape a drought at Bethel. Joseph drove his chariot over them, and Moses was a familiar figure there for 40 years. But today, Memphis is a mere wilderness of palms and fallen statuary. This colossal statue of Rameses II has thrown itself across "Broadway", so to speak, as if to say, STOP!

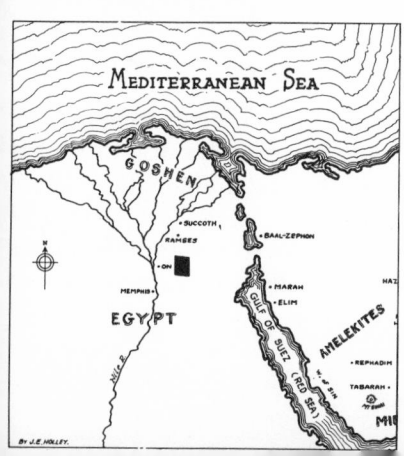

193— THE OBELISK HELIOPOLIS (ON)

Now we cross the Nile to Heliopolis, ancient On. Joseph took the daughter of the Priest of On as his wife, and they became the parents of Ephraim and Manasseh, (Gen. 41.) The Holy Family also is said to have camped here during their sojourn in Egypt, when they fled from Herod. A companion of this beautiful obelisk, now stands at the entrance of Central Park in New York City.

194— THE LAND OF GOSHEN

The most fertile portion of the Nile delta is Goshen. The sons of Jacob (Israel), and brothers of Joseph, cultivated these productive acres, which were set apart for them by Pharoah, for Joseph's sake. After Joseph died, Israel was enslaved, her children murdered at birth, Moses was born, and the Passover was inaugurated in this very soil. (Ex. 12.)

195— THE RED SEA

Israel's position in Egypt became so intolerable that God came to their rescue in a special way. The night of the Passover, they fled to the Red Sea, and when Pharaoh's hosts pressed down upon them, the Sea opened and Israel walked over on dry ground. The shore over there is Baal-Zephon, and marks the beginning place of 40 years in the Wilderness. (Exodus 14.)

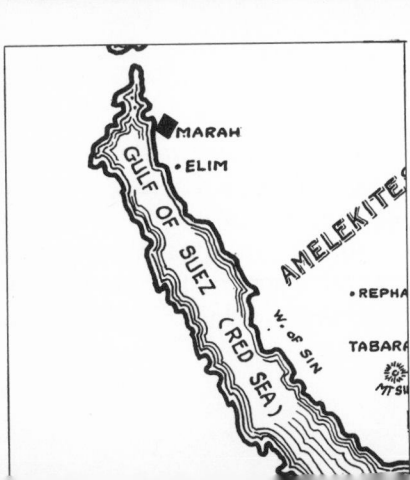

196— MARRAH

It seemed that Moses started to "The Promised Land" through the Wilderness of Shur, but they turned back from Shur, and their first stop was here at Marrah (Bitter Water). But Moses sweetened the water by casting a certain kind of tree into it, which Israel accepted as a great miracle, and which it likely was. (Exodus 15:23.) (See map.)

197— ELIM

Next, Israel moved to Elim, a few miles south of Marrah, where they found 12 gushing fountains of water, and a great forest of palm trees; they halted here for several days. And the people took courage after their bitter experience at Marrah. As we pass over this desolate region, bear in mind that Israel numbered a million, or more, who had to be fed—the greatest miracle of all time. (Ex. 16.)

198— THE WILDERNESS OF SIN

Now they move to the Wilderness of Sin, where the parched ground never produced a blade of grass, because it "never rains." And it so happened at this point, their food supply became exhausted. So Providence stepped in again. The "manna fell" and they were bombarded by a shower of quail, which temporarily solved their problem. (Exodus 16.)

199— REPHIDIM

Their next stop was at Rephidim, where Israel encountered more difficulties. Here they were attacked by the Amalikites, (whose progenitor was Abraham, through his wife, Keturah). (Gen. 25:1.) And there was no water. So the Lord interferred again; the enemy was driven away and fountains of water broke forth from the flinty rock, and they were saved. (Ex. 16.)

200— SINAI (SHEPHERD)

Rephidim is in sight of Sinai, where the greatest event in Israel's experience occurred. Moses is on familiar ground here, for he had been shepherd of Jethro's flocks around this mountain for 40 years. While thus engaged, Moses witnessed "The Burning Bush" out on this plain, and met Aaron, his brother, who accompanied him when he led their brethren out of Egypt. (Exodus 2.)

201— MOUNT SINAI

Here is the great mountain of flint, Mt. Sinai, which extends itself skyward 8,000 feet. Moses went into this mountain and got the tables of stone, while Israel camped here on the plain below. After he returned with the second tablets, he constructed the Tabernacle, built the Ark of the Covenant, and they remained here 325 days. (Exodus 19.)

202—VALLEY OF JETHRO

Jethro, father-in-law of Moses, once lived in this majestic valley, then called "Jethro's Pass," but now, "St. Catherine's Monastery." From here he must have climbed the mountain many times, while the thunder roared from the clouds which hovered about its summit. But now he is to scale its peaks again, but for an entirely different purpose.

203— MOSES' CHAPEL

Since his shepherd days, Moses has seen the "Burning Bush," and heard the voice of the "Great I AM." This time he is ascending Sinai to talk with God. In this silent wilderness of granite, he received "The Tables of Stone," "The Ten Commandments," and this unpretentious Chapel is said to mark the spot where he spent those 40 memorable days. (Ex. 19-20.)

204— HILL OF AARON

When Moses returned to the plain below—this very mound —he found Israel dancing around "A Golden Calf," cast by his brother, Aaron. He was so bewildered by the disgraceful sight that he destroyed the Tablets, ground the image to powder, which he mixed with water, and made them drink it. Moses then got new Tablets, and remained here nearly a year.

205— ELIJAH'S CHAPEL

Elijah also fasted 40 days in Sinai, when he escaped the wrath of Jezebel. He came here to receive instructions from God, and finally heard "The Still Small Voice," which gave him comfort and certainty. So on the slopes of this sacred mountain, this Chapel has been erected to commemorate the event. (1 Kings 19.)

206— HILL OF THE BURNING BUSH

It was while Moses was serving Jethro as shepherd that he decided to return to Egypt and emancipate his brethren in slavery. Out of a "Burning Bush," a "Voice," identifying itself as "The Great I AM," gave him full directions and authority to proceed. So from this spot he began his task to deliver Israel. This is the "Hill of the Burning Bush." (Exodus 3.)

207— TRAMMEL NETS

The first camp of Israel, after leaving Sinai, was Taberah, where many were consumed by fire. At Hazeroth, Miriam was stricken with leprosy, and here at Kibroth-Hattaavah, the quail flew over again and many gluttons died. With the regularity as well timed as the swallows at Capistrano, quail return annually to Sinai. "Trammel Nets" like this, are set up, and the birds fall against them and drift high, and the markets of Jerusalem and Cairo are glutted with them. (Num. 11.)

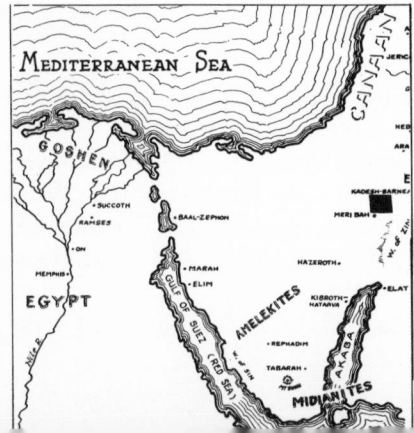

208— KADESH-BARNEA

The cloud lifted and Moses moved on to Kadesh-Barnea. The Twelve Spies were sent out from here. Israel remained at Kadesh-Barnea for 35 years. They suffered privations, many were destroyed by plagues, and Miriam died. (Num. 20:1.) After this, Israel moved out to Meribah, where Moses and Aaron struck the rock again and water flowed as it had done at Rephidim. Then came the fiery reptiles and Moses raised the "Brazen Serpent." (Num. 13-14.)

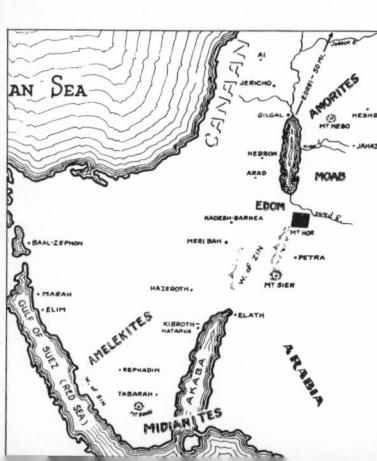

209— MOUNT HOR

A little way from Meribah, Israel camped again at the foot of Mt. Hor, a rather ugly looking mountain, which seems to have been disfavored by nature. Here they were attacked by the Aradites, a people near Hebron, where the 12 spies seemed to have trespassed on them many years before. But the enemy was beaten off and there was not a general war. (Num. 20.)

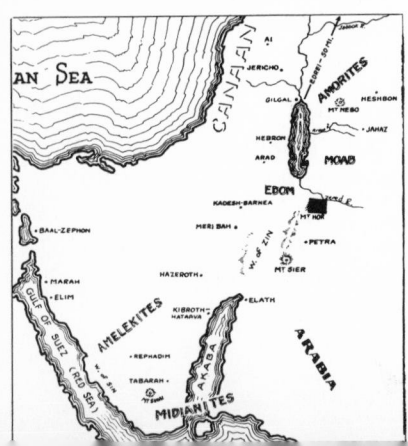

210— AARON'S TOMB

And Aaron, discouraged with it all, deliberately ascended Mt. Hor, accompanied by Moses, and died. And this is his tomb. So Aaron, Israel's first High Priest, finished his life's work here, where his tomb is seldom visited or seen by human eyes. The office of High Priest was then delivered to Eleazar, his son, who carried on from here.

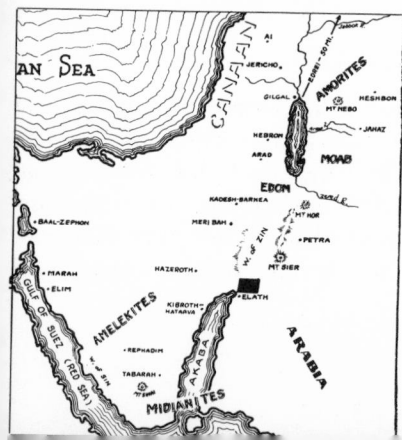

211— ELATH (AKABA)

When Moses applied to Edom (Esau) for permission to pass through their territory, they flatly refused. However, Moab (Lot) acted favorably, and Israel moved to Elath and surrounded Edom. Complaints again became maddening, and fiery serpents attacked the people, and Moses lifted up the "Brazen Serpent," and the dying people were saved. (Deut. 2.) (See map.)

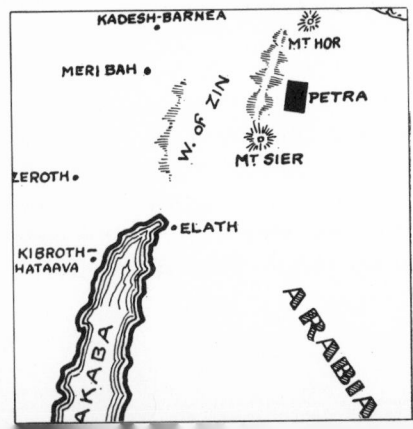

212—PETRA (ROCK) HILLS

The route taken by Moses led him through, or near by Petra, a place, though not mentioned in the Bible, is so interesting that we must see a bit of it. The entire region was originally like this: cliffs and crags, and canyons, streaked with various pleasing colors, but because there was nothing to subsist on, it has no population today. (Map.)

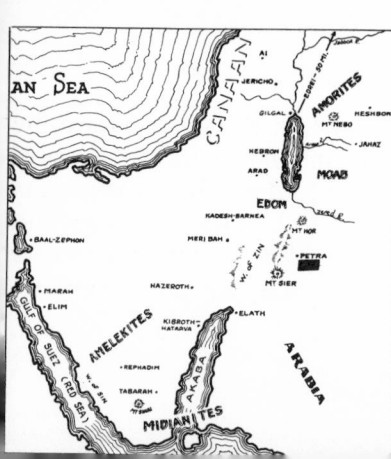

213— THE THEATRE

Petra is the most unique ghost city in the world, and we may guess with certainty that there was a very large population here at one time. Not only does the immensity of the construction favor the fact, but here is a theatre which accommodated multitudes, which would not have been here had there been no people to patronize it.

214— THE HIGH PLACE

Did the Edomites build it? They were a nomadic people. Did Egypt build it? What resemblance does it bear to the Sphinx or the Pyramids? If traders used it as a crossroad and each made his contribution, then they all used the same "Altar of Sacrifice," which is unthinkable. It is all a deep mystery, and one's guess is as good as another's.

215— EL-KAZNE

The El-Kazne is the most beautiful example of workmanship here. It is not built up against the mountain, but is chiseled out of the mountain itself, and stands out in bold relief like a huge vari-colored cameo. Neither are the rooms built in, but are cut out in the solid rock, as a tunnel is cut through a rocky hill. In all the world, there is nothing like it.

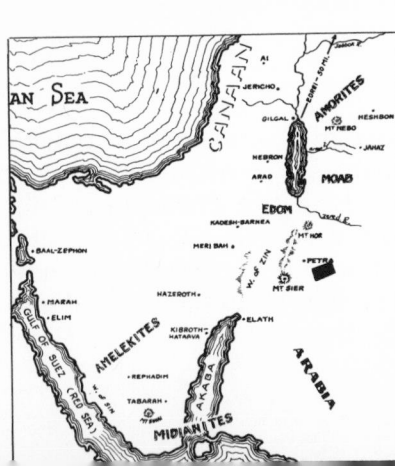

216— ED-DEIR

The Ed-Deir is much larger than El-Kazne, as you can see from the comparative size of the man in the entrance. Nearly 200 feet above the entrance, the top is ornamented by a great stone urn, 30 or more feet in diameter, and is called the "Treasury of Pharaoh" by the natives. It is all beautiful, baffling and stupendous.

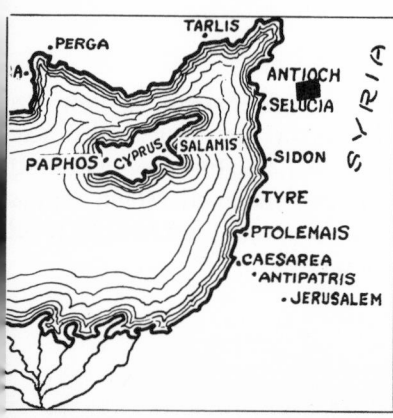

217— ANTIOCH

There are other outlying places that should be brought into this story, so we are making a journey of more than 300 miles to Antioch, beyond Ancient Phoenicia on the River Orontes. The Disciples were first called Christians in Antioch (Acts 11:36). The first Gentile Church was located here, and the first foreign Missionaries, Paul and Barnabas, were sent out by the Antioch Church. (Acts 13:1.) (Map locates it.)

218— SIDON (AIR)

From Antioch we drop down the Mediterranean shore to Sidon in Phoenicia. In the days of Ahab, one Ethbaal was King and Priest of Sidon, and his daughter was Jezebel, who became Ahab's wife, and who hated Elijah. Jesus preached and healed in Phoenicia, and Paul landed here and called on the Church. (Acts 27:3.)

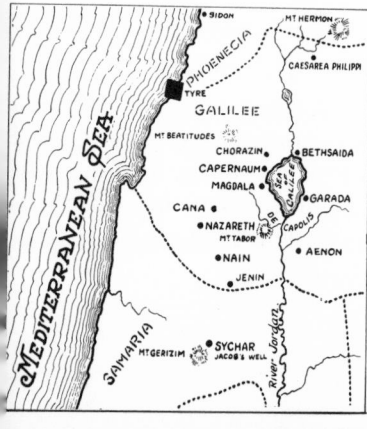

219— TYRE — HIRAM'S TOMB

In the days of David, Hiram was King of Tyre, and a good friend of David. Hiram of Tyre furnished many workmen who supplied the timbers for Solomon's Temple, which were cut from the forests near Tyre. (1 Kings 5:1.) This is Hiram's tomb. Jesus also preached and healed near here and Paul spent seven days here with the Church, while he was en route from Ephesus to Jerusalem, on his last trip there. (Acts 21:3.)

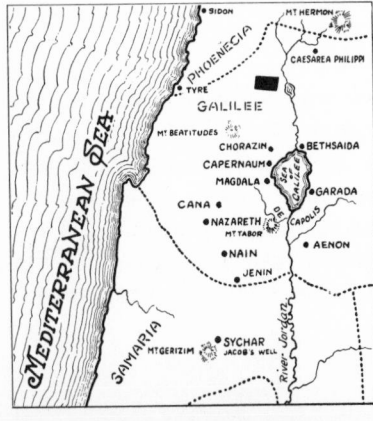

220— HAZOR

Here is where Hazor once stood, near Lake Hulah (Waters of Merom). Hazor is the only city ever destroyed by fire by Joshua. In the days of Deborah, its King was Jabin. He sent Sisera to the Kishon, where his army was totally destroyed and his own life was taken by a woman, Jael, at Megiddo. (Joshua 11:12.)

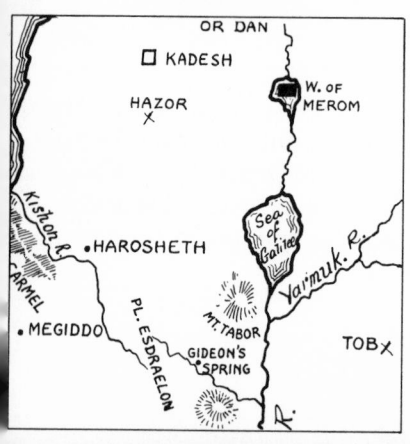

221— WATERS OF MEROM

This beautiful little body of water, nestled among the foothills of Mt. Hermon, is called Lake Hulah. It is merely a wide place in the Jordan, and can be waded at any point. It is on sea level. Sometime in the past, the Red Sea, 250 miles south, extended to this point; the Dead Sea was 1300 feet deeper than it now is, and there was no River Jordan, or Sea of Galilee, at all. (See map.)

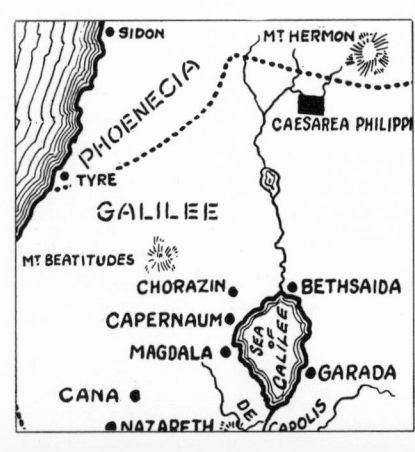

222— CAESAREA-PHILIPPI

After Jesus had healed the Blind Man at Bethsaida-Julius, he spent a week here at Caesarea-Philippi, located at the foot of Mt. Hermon. It was here that Peter confessed that "Jesus is the Christ;" and it so pleased Jesus that he pronounced the greatest blessing on him that heaven has to offer. (Luke 9:18.)

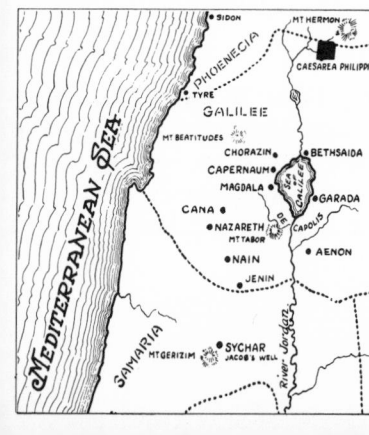

223— CAESAREA-PHILIPPI GATE

We are now at the entrance of Caesarea Philippi, which was built by Philip, and was named for the Emperor and himself. The bridge in front of us crosses the little stream-let, Jordan, and enters the city gate. You will remember that it was Philip's wife who was living with his brother, Antipas, at Tiberias, and his daughter, Salome, whose vulgar dance purchased the head of John the Baptist.

224— SOURCE OF JORDAN

A short distance north of Caesarea-Philippi, this great Spring bursts forth from the side of Mt. Hermon and it forms, or is, the source of that sacred River. Mt. Hermon is directly above us and Jesus may have begun his ascent of the mountain right here.

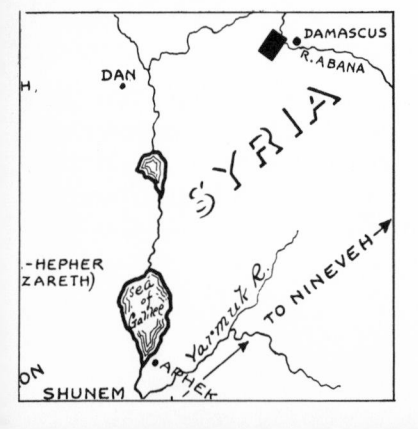

225— RIVER PHARPAR

And here is the River Pharpar on the opposite (east) side of Mt. Hermon. Naaman, the leper, told Elisha, when the Prophet demanded him to go dip himself in the Jordan, and he would be healed, that its waters were much superior to those of the Jordan. Before us stands the mighty Hermon lifting its summit 10,000 feet into the clouds. The Transfiguration of Jesus was witnessed in that mountain, where he met Moses and Elijah face to face, and his disciples heard the Voice of God say: "Hear My Son." (2 Kings 5.)

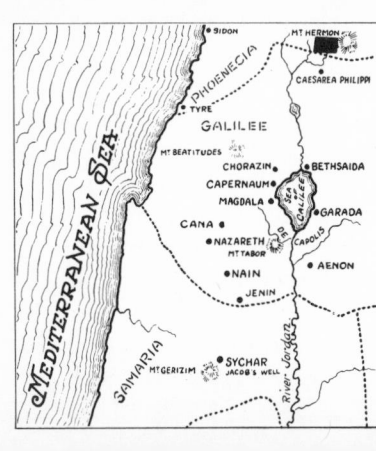

226– MT. HERMON SUNRISE

We have seen Mt. Hermon at a distance, from various points several times, but now we give you an experience few people have ever enjoyed: to witness a sunrise from its very summit. It is not presumed that Jesus and the Disciples came this far when they met Moses and Elijah, and it was far below that Jesus healed the mentally deranged boy. (Luke 9:37.)

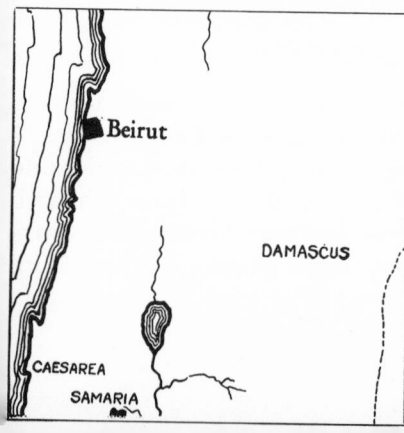

227— BEIRUT

Beirut is not mentioned in the Bible, but undoubtedly it has some connection, perhaps under some other name; but it is the capital of Lebanon and a port of entry into the Middle East. It is the seat of the great American University (from which this picture was made), and its influence is felt for thousands of miles in every direction.

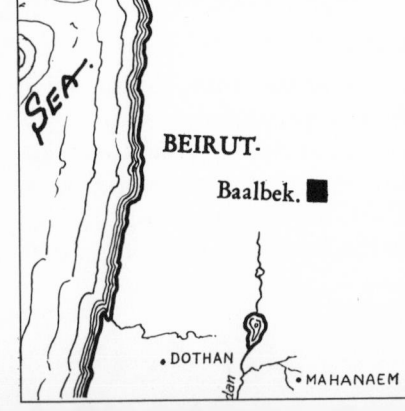

228— BAALBECK RUINS

Between Beirut and Damascus are the old and elaborate ruins of a civilization which flourished many centuries ago —Ballbeck. The entire surroundings are so bewildering that one gets lost in thought as he moves among the stupendous ruins, about which little or nothing is known. This graceful and perfect group of columns, Temple of the Sun, is only one in the acres of ruins surrounding it. (Map.)

229— THE GRAND QUARRY

In the distance you see that majestic ruins again which once had its place along side its companions, like this. This tremendous stone was intended to have a place in a similar structure, but something must have happened when the masons got this far with it, or the building campaign suddenly stopped. Compare the man with the great stone.

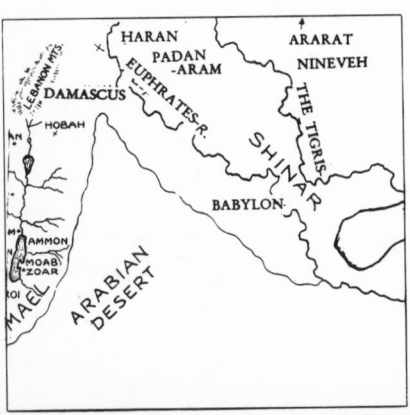

230— ABANA AT DAMASCUS

Now we come to Damascus, one of the two oldest cities in the world, and here is the historic Abana River that flows through it, gives it life and makes Damascus what it is—no Abana, no Damascus. Its history extends from Abraham to Paul, and it still stands until this day. It is a grand old city and brimful of interest. (2 Kings 5.)

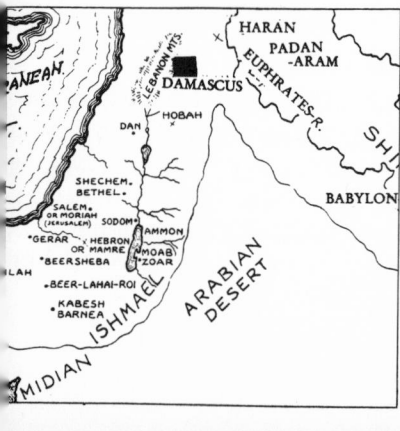

231– "STREET CALLED STRAIGHT"

The light line stretching across the city here is the "Street Called Straight." It is glazed over for a long distance, and displays a beautiful effect, but by no means makes the place any cooler. Judas, a disciple of Damascus, lived down that street somewhere and the blinded Paul was led to his place, where he waited further instructions, which came from one Ananias, a disciple of Damascus. (Acts 9:11.)

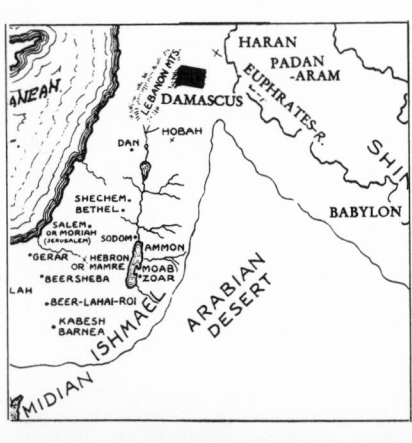

232— DAMASCUS WALL

Saul apparently was so enthusiastic about his experience with Christ in the way, that he evidently told it with great emphasis, and perhaps to avoid trouble with the Jews, he went into seclusion in Arabia. (Gal. 1:17.) Upon his return, the Jews were so offended at his teaching, that finally the brethren planned his escape, and lowered him from this wall in a basket. (Acts 9.)

233— HOUSE OF NAAMAN (Ruins)

Naaman, the leper, also lived in Damascus and here are the ruins of his residence. For many years the property has been devoted to the housing of lepers, and there are many of them. However, the majority of them prefer to be at liberty and beg, rather than occupy the quarters furnished by the Government. (2 Kings 5.)

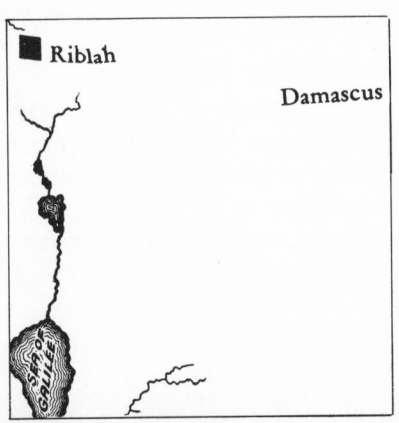

234— RIBLAH

Near the source of the Orontes, north of Damascus, is the city of Riblah. Zedekiah, the last King of Judah, was brought here, a prisoner, by Nebuchadnezzar after the fall of Jerusalem. Zedekiah was compelled to witness the horrible murder of his sons, then his eyes were "bored out" and he was driven to Babylon. (2 Kings 25.)

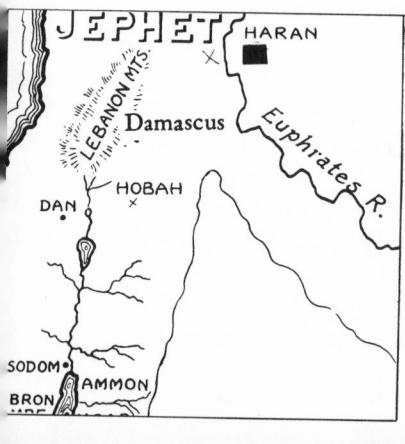

235— HARAN

Now we move to what might well be named the unknown land—Haran—in far off Padan-Aram. Terah, father of Abraham, came here from Ur of the Chaldees and died at the age of 205. Haran was the home of Rebecca, wife of Isaac, and also the home of Jacob's wife, Rachel, whose tomb we saw at Bethlehem. Jacob met her at the Well at Haran. (Map.)

236— THE HARAN MILL

The Padan-Aram country is barren. The soil is fertile enough, but the rainfall is almost zero. Why, with the abundance of water from the mighty Tigris and Euphrates, is this gadget not supplanted by great mills, like those in Minneapolis and St. Paul? Some day a system of irrigation will be installed that will make this "desert blossom as a rose."

237— TOMB OF JONAH (NINEVEH)

Nineveh, once the capital and world metropolis, has been ravaged and destroyed time and again. But the memory of at least one man has been kept alive—Jonah—and the Minaret marks his tomb. Jonah was divinely commissioned to preach here. He tried to run away from the Lord, and was "swallowed by a whale." His message was "repent or perish," and they repented. (Book of Jonah.)

238— BAGDAD

Situated on the refreshing Tigris; and more beautiful because of the semi-arid country surrounding it, is the quaint and magnificent city of Bagdad. It is the grand metropolis of Iraq and is well worth a stay of several days. But since it has no place in the Bible story, we merely pass it on our way to Babylon.

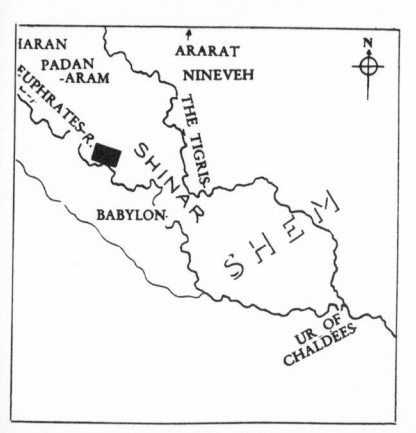

239— THE EUPHRATES RIVER

The Tigris and Euphrates parallel each other for a long distance. So now we will cross the narrow strip of land between them, and here is the mighty Euphrates. At this point it probably looks just like it did when Noah and Nimrod wandered up and down its shores. Any native will proudly respond: "Yes, Sir, this was once the Garden of Eden." In fact, nature, unaided, tries to force her idea of plenty on the shiftless populace, but they are not interested.

240— RUINS OF BABYLON

This is Babylon as you see it today, and there are acres and acres just like it that you cannot see. The only living creatures occupying the palaces of Nebuchadnezzar and Belshazzar, are owls and bats. Once the greatest city on earth, where every kind of sound, from music to merriment, to the screams of those who were being murdered, met your ear, now only a deathly silence reigns. (Daniel.)

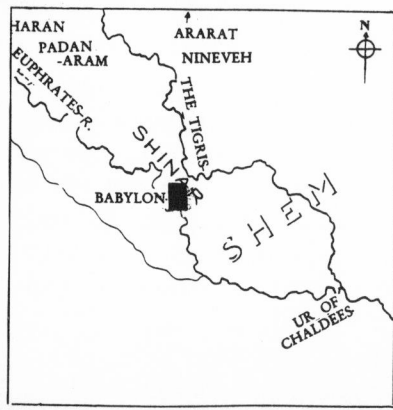

241— VIA SACRA

This was the "Pennsylvania Avenue" of Babylon. Nebuchadnezzar strutted down this boulevard leading the eyeless Zedekiah by a rope around his neck, and the gruesome procession was applauded by the multitudes that lined the street. The Medes and Persians also marched down this street in their victory parade, the night of Belshazzar's drunken brawl in the palace, and Babylon fell.

242— ISHTAR GATE

Nebuchadnezzar's banquet hall was entered through the Ishtar Gate, where, later, the drunken Belshazzar saw the hand-writing on the wall, which read: "You are weighed in the balance, and found wanting!" You can still see the relief work on the walls, which were then covered with gold—a city of bewildering beauty.

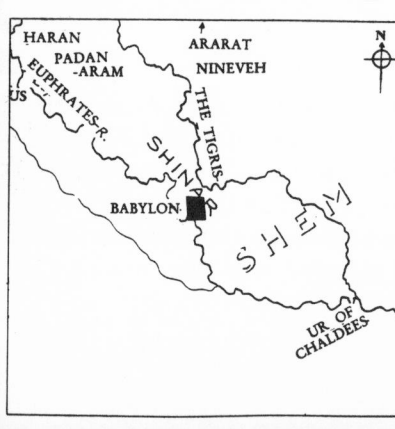

243— LION OF BABYLON

The statue of the lion, here, stands over the spot where Daniel was cast into a lion's den. This is the great black basalt lion portraying the fate of victims cast into the Lion's Den. But not so in the case of Daniel, for he had something, or knew something, that others did not have —a knowledge of God. (Daniel 6.)

244— BIRS NIMROD

South of Babylon, this great mount, and disintegrating tower, is pointed out as the ancient "Tower of Babel." So 5,000 years ago we might have seen "The Mighty Nimrod" attempting to build a tower that would reach to heaven. But when their "language was confounded," it halted the work, and they finally abandoned the undertaking. (Gen. 11.)

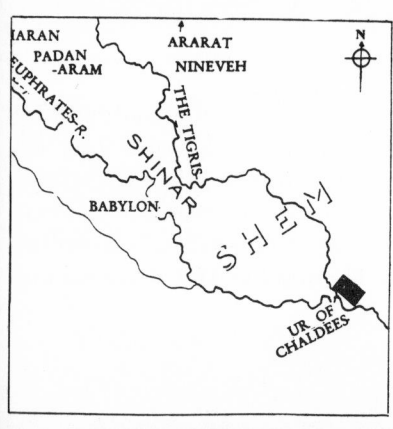

245— UR OF THE CHALDEES

These ruins bespeak the day, 50 or 60 centuries ago, when ancient Ur of the Chaldees stood on these foundations. At no great distance from this spot, lived Terah, an idol maker, whose son was Abraham, and whose daughter was Sarah. The father died at Haran, at the age of 205, as we have seen; and Abraham, who had married Sarah, moved on to Canaan. (Gen. 11:24-32.)

246— SHRINE OF ABRAHAM

Although Abraham spent only a fraction of his life in this Chaldean region, his name still lingers in the hearts of the Chaldeans, and this shrine has been dedicated to him. Abraham died in Hebron—a great distance from here. "Abraham gave up the ghost, and died in a good, old age, an old man, and full of years, and was gathered to his people." (Gen. 25:8.)

247— EUPHRATES SUNSET

As we stand on the shore of the great Euphrates, we are reminded of the day when Daniel and Ezekiel kept the thought of God before the Jews until they whispered: "By the rivers of Babylon, there we sat down, yea, we wept when we remembered Zion. We hanged our harps upon the willows in the midst thereof, For there they that carried us away captive required of us a song." (Psalm 137.)

248— SHRINE OF EZEKIEL

The solemn chant may have been led by Ezekiel, and the people responded: "If I forget thee, O Jerusalem, Let my right hand forget her cunning. If I do not remember thee, let my tongue cleave to the roof of my mouth." Ezekiel never got back to Jerusalem, he passed on from the land of the Euphrates. And this is his tomb, or shrine, in that far away land.

INDEX